$5 Dollar Menus for Two

$5 Dollar Menus For Two

Sylvia Bennett

BIG APPLE VISION BOOKS
An Imprint of Big Apple Vision Publishers

BIG APPLE VISION BOOKS
An Imprint of Big Apple Vision Publishers, New York

Copyright © 2003 by Sylvia Bennett
ISBN 0-9724327-7-9
www.bigapplevision.com

First Big Apple Vision Books hardcover printing: April 2004

Big Apple Vision™ is a registered trademark of Big Apple Vision Publishing, Inc.

Printed in Canada

On the cover: A&B Aubergine à la Cairo
recipe, on page 186-187

Library of Congress Cataloging-in-Publication Data

ACKNOWLEDGEMENTS

This cookbook was enthusiastically created for all those people, who like me, have been yearning for a healthy way to experience the art of preparing and enjoying food.

Each recipe contained in this cookbook will assist you in creating the perfect match between food chemistry and body chemistry as detailed in Eleonora DeLennart's popular book, *The BioChemical Machine.*

Enjoy preparing the recipes,
Savor the eating experience,
And most importantly, take pleasure in good health.

sb

CONTENTS

Introduction

Eating is life affirming. It plays an instrumental role in the creation of good health, plentiful energy, lasting beauty and pure joy. To live well is to eat well. At least this should be the case. However, the truth is that this most basic of human needs is often linked to many of today's most pressing health problems. For many, the joy in eating has been supplanted by the guilt, fear and concerns of becoming overweight, ill and fatigued. Alas, the enjoyment of eating has been transformed into a stressful deprivation driven largely by the misguided and misinformed recommendations of an obsolete diet industry.

And there is cooking, one of humankind's greatest discoveries and most treasured arts. But for many, the fears of illness and obesity have reduced this cherished art to little more than what I call the "Don't-Don't" mentality. (Don't Eat This, Don't Eat That)

$5 Menus for Two strives to accomplish two important goals. First, to restore the traditional joys associated with preparing and eating favorite foods. And secondly, to eliminate the guilt, and negative impact of these foods on the body by providing specific menus that will help you create the perfect match of food chemistry and body chemistry. This is called the A&B Method, which was introduced in Eleonora DeLennart's popular book, *The BioChemical Machine*.

The A&B Method should be a family affair. Since *$5 Menus for Two* focuses on the laws of chemistry and not deprivation, you and your family can return to eating your favorite foods without obsessing over category or quantity. You can even drink beer, wine, and liquor because this is about the natural laws of chemistry and not the unnatural laws of the diet industry.

Even though it is not part of this book, I strongly recommend you begin each day eating apples with milk or yogurt. Not only will this satisfy your hunger for many hours, it will provide your body with a rich supply of the essential nutrients it needs each day.

I have adhered to this practice over the past 10 years and I am living proof of its merit. My weight has remained the same. I rarely if ever get sick. And last but not least, I have kept my looks and the youthful texture of my skin.

$5 Menus for Two (and The A&B Method) is for everybody. Not only the lucky few who can afford to pay exorbitant prices for the prepared foods associated with the latest fad diet. I created this cookbook so that everyone will be able to once again cook happy, eat happy and most importantly, live happy.

Enjoy!

Using This Cookbook

Since there are no "hard and fast" rules for following the A&B principles other than doing your best to avoid eating A and B foods at the same meal, it's up to you to decide whether your menu will be based on A or B foods. If you have read *The BioChemical Machine*, you already know that the Neutrals fit beautifully with any A, B, or other Neutral food. And of course the best part of the Neutrals is that they can be eaten at any time, 24 hours 7 days a week.

If you are currently experiencing serious health problems, you should first speak with your doctor to determine which of these recipes are right for your particular ailment. Keep in mind to always add the A&B Power Salad to whatever menu you choose to ensure your system receives all the essential vitamins and minerals, vital for your well being.

"Neutrals"
The A&B Freebies

Neutral Soups

French A&B Pea Soup

2 cups green peas
2/3 cup butter, diced
6 cups chicken bouillon
1 cup heavy cream
Sea salt to taste
Freshly ground white pepper to taste

1. Soak peas for at least 1 hour. Put peas in a food processor, mix until puree.
2. In a stockpot, heat chicken bouillon, add puree. Bring to a boil. Season it with sea salt and ground white pepper to taste.
3. Beat in the butter and heavy cream. Serve warm.

Oriental A&B Lentil Soup

1-1/2 cups lentils, dried
2 cups vegetable or chicken bouillon (or cubes)
8 cups (distilled) water
1 large onion, minced
1 clove garlic, crushed through a press
2 stalks celery, chopped
2 large carrots, chopped
2 tablespoons fresh parsley, chopped
1/2 teaspoon dried thyme
1/2 teaspoon sea salt
3 tablespoons olive oil
1 teaspoon dried oregano
1 teaspoon sweet Hungarian paprika

1. In a stockpot, heat oil over medium-high setting. Add onions, tossing for 5 minutes, until crisp-tender.
2. Add garlic, carrots and celery. Add seasoning and herbs; mix well, tossing for 3–4 minutes.
3. Add vegetable or chicken bouillon; cook for 3 minutes.
4. Add lentils and 8 cups water. Simmer over low heat for about 60 minutes; add parsley. Serve warm.

Prussian A&B Crème Soup

6 cups carrots, chopped
5 large shallots, minced
1/2 cup minced onion
3 tablespoons butter
8 cups chicken bouillon
1 tablespoon dried dill
1/2 cup heavy cream
Sea salt to taste
Pepper to taste

1. In a stockpot, heat butter over medium heat. Sauté shallots until tender. Add carrots, cook for another 10 minutes.
2. Add 8 cups bouillon, bring to a simmer; cook until carrots are tender.
3. Put soup in a blender (or use a hand blender) and let cook on medium heat. Add sea salt, pepper, dill and cream to taste. Serve warm.

Creamy
A&B Cauliflower Soup

6 cups (distilled) water
2 medium cauliflowers, cored and coarsely chopped
1 onion, chopped
1 clove garlic, crushed through a press
2 tablespoons butter
1 tablespoon olive oil
2 stalks celery, chopped
8 scallions, chopped
2 tablespoons vegetable bouillon (or bouillon cubes)
1/8 teaspoon black pepper
1/8 teaspoon nutmeg
1 teaspoon dried basil
1/2 teaspoon dried thyme
1 teaspoon dried marjoram
1/2 teaspoon celery or sea salt

1. In a large saucepan, melt butter and heat oil. Add scallions, onions, garlic, cauliflower and celery. Season with salt and pepper to taste. Cook over medium heat for several minutes, stirring frequently.
2. Add water and bouillon; bring to a boil. Add basil, thyme and marjoram. Simmer, covered, over medium heat until cauliflower is tender, for 10–15 minutes.

3. Remove cover and cool slightly. In blender, process until soup is smooth and creamy. Repeat; add nutmeg to taste. Serve warm.

Neutral
Hors d'oeuvres
& Appetizers

Mozzarella with Tomatoes

2 large tomatoes, sliced
1 ball mozzarella, sliced
Fresh basil
Vinegar to taste
Olive oil to taste
Salt to taste
Pepper to taste

1. Cut tomatoes and mozzarella into thin slices. Arrange on a platter or serving plate.
2. In a small bowl, combine vinegar and oil. Pour mixture over mozzarella and tomatoes. Add salt and pepper to taste. Garnish with fresh basil.

A&B Avocados

1 large avocado (1/2 for every person)
4 tablespoons lemon juice
1 bunch dill, chopped
4 tablespoons olive oil
Salt to taste
Pepper to taste

1. Using a sharp knife, cut avocado in halves. Remove pit.
2. In a medium bowl, combine lemon juice, oil, salt, and pepper to taste. Mix well.
3. Top with dill. Pour mixture over avocado and dill. Serve immediately, or cover with plastic wrap to prevent avocado from darkening. Refrigerate.

Smoked Salmon

Salmon, sliced (quantity to taste)
Fresh dill, chopped
Whipped cream, fresh
Fresh lemon juice

1. Place salmon on a large plate.
2. Top salmon with fresh whipped cream. Sprinkle with lemon juice and dill evenly.

A&B Salads

There is no limit on the quantity of vegetables, salads, sprouts, and herbs you may eat. Since variety is important, you may freely substitute any vegetable especially root vegetables like carrots, turnips, and beets. These are the best choices for the purpose of detoxifying the body along with such vegetables like spinach, beet tops, chard, celery, onion tops, watercress, broccoli, cauliflower, sprouts, and all other green vegetables that contains juice.

A&B Power Salad

Lettuce (romaine, iceberg, limestone, red leaf, watercress,
        or any other lettuce, broken into bite-size pieces)
Tomatoes, sliced or diced into cubes
Cucumber, sliced or diced into cubes
Carrots, chopped or sliced
Cauliflower, chopped
Broccoli, chopped
White and/or red cabbage, chopped
Sprouts/soy sprouts
Spinach, chopped
Onions, sliced or diced into cubes
Scallions, sliced
Parsley, chopped
Chives, chopped
Oil to taste (olive, flaxseed, sesame, etc.)
Apple vinegar (opt: Balsamic) or fresh lemon juice to taste
Salt (sea salt, herb salt, Bio-salt) to taste
Pepper to taste

1. Cut up vegetables. In a large bowl, combine all vegetables.
2. In a small bowl, combine oil, vinegar, salt, pepper, and chives.

OPTIONAL: salad dressing, chunky blue cheese dressing, mayonnaise or dip/dressing. Pour over salad.

A&B Classic Green Salad

1 head lettuce—butter, red leaf, iceberg, or romaine
  (washed, dried, and sliced into bite-sized pieces)
1 small cucumber, peeled and sliced
2 tomatoes, sliced
3 carrots, sliced
1 large onion, sliced
2 garlic cloves, crushed through a press
3 tablespoons olive oil
1 tablespoon fresh lemon juice or vinegar
1/4 – 1/2 teaspoon sea salt
1/2 teaspoon celery salt

Place all ingredients in a bowl. Pour dressing over salad and toss well.

A&B Ramses Salad

5–6 fresh hot peppers, such as jalapenos
2 large tomatoes
2 large onions
1 head lettuce
6 cloves garlic
1/2 cup vinegar
1/2 cup olive oil
1 tablespoon coriander
1 bunch cilantro
1 tablespoon cumin
Salt to taste
Pepper to taste

In a food processor, combine peppers, tomatoes, onions, lettuce, garlic, salt, pepper, vinegar, oil, and herbs. Process until well blended. Ideal with fava beans (see recipe "Ramses Beans"), whole wheat bread, or steamed potatoes.

A&B Asparagus Salad

1 head lettuce
1/2 head red leaf lettuce
1/2 pound fresh (or canned) asparagus
3 tablespoons olive oil
1 tablespoon vinegar
Lemon juice to taste
1/2 teaspoon mustard
1 clove garlic, crushed through a press
Sea salt to taste
Fresh ground black pepper

1. Wash lettuce; dry and break into pieces. Break and discard heavy ends from asparagus.
2. In a medium saucepan, cook asparagus and salt in boiling salted water until tender, 3–5 minutes. Remove from water. Drain well. Cut into 1-1/2-inch pieces. Combine with lettuce.
3. For dressing, combine oil, mustard, sea salt, and lemon juice (and/or vinegar). Add pepper to taste. Mix well. Pour over salad.

A&B Celery Salad

1 medium bunch of celery
1/2 cup mayonnaise
2 tablespoons fresh lemon juice or vinegar
2 teaspoons mustard
Seasoning to taste

1. Cut celery into very thin slices. Cut peel from slices; then julienne each slice. Add lemon juice.
2. Place celery in boiling water for 3–5 minutes until tender. Drain well. Combine mayonnaise and mustard. Toss celery in mixture. Season to taste. Serve at room temperature.

A&B Carrot Salad

1 pound large carrots
Olive oil to taste
Lemon (or vinegar) to taste
Dash garlic salt
Dash pepper
Dash artificial sweetener

In a processor, slice carrots into 1/8-inch slices. Add remaining ingredients. Mix well. Serve on lettuce.

A&B Cucumber with Dill

4 cucumbers, peeled and sliced
1 cup sour cream
2 tablespoons fresh lemon juice or apple vinegar
2 tablespoons fresh dill, chopped, or 1 tablespoon dried dill
1/4 teaspoon sea salt
1 teaspoon scallions, minced

Combine ingredients. Mix well.

Neutral Mayonnaise, Salad Dressings, & Dips

A&B Remoulade Dressing

1 cup mayonnaise
2 tablespoons horseradish

In a bowl, combine mayonnaise and horseradish. Stir until well blended.

A&B Classic Mayonnaise

2 egg yolks (*)
2 tablespoons olive oil
1 lemon juice or vinegar
Salt to taste

In a bowl, combine ingredients (which must be refrigerated first). Add drop by drop 2 tablespoons olive oil and lemon juice. Whisk until well blended. Refrigerate until firm.

(*) *The quantity alters for 4 egg yolks, by 8 tablespoons olive oil, lemon juice, salt, and 5 tablespoons water. There is some danger of salmonella from uncooked egg yolks.*

A&B French Garlic Mayonnaise

5 egg yolks (*)
5 tablespoon olive oil
5 tablespoon (filtered) water
1 lemon juice or vinegar
6 clove of garlic, crushed through a press
Salt to taste

Combine ingredients (must be refrigerated first). Add drop by drop 5 tablespoons oil. Add lemon juice drop by drop as well. Add garlic and salt to taste. Whisk until well blended. Refrigerate until firm.

(*) *There is some danger of salmonella from uncooked egg yolks.*

A&B Chili Mayonnaise

1/2 cup mayonnaise
2 teaspoons chili powder
1 teaspoon ground cumin
2 teaspoons fresh lemon juice or vinegar
Dash salt
1/8 teaspoon cayenne pepper

In a small bowl, combine ingredients, except mayonnaise. Stir until well blended. Blend in mayonnaise.

A&B French Spicy Mayonnaise

1 cup mayonnaise
1 hard-boiled egg yolk, mashed
1 tablespoon chopped anchovies
1 tablespoon chopped parsley
1 tablespoon drained capers
1 teaspoon mustard
Dash cayenne pepper

In a small bowl, combine all ingredients. Stir until well blended. Cover and refrigerate.

A&B Oriental Curry-Lemon Mayonnaise

1/2 cup mayonnaise
1/2 cup sour cream
1-1/2 teaspoons curry powder
1 tablespoon fresh lemon juice or vinegar
Dash salt
Dash cayenne pepper

1. In a small bowl, combine mayonnaise and sour cream. Mix until well blended. Stir in lemon juice, salt, and cayenne. Add curry powder.
2. Cover and refrigerate.

A&B Creamy Avocado Dressing

1 avocado
1 clove garlic, crushed through a press
2 teaspoons olive oil
1/4 cup water
2 tablespoons sour cream
1 tablespoon fresh (or dried) dill
1/2 teaspoon sea salt
2 tablespoons lemon juice (or vinegar)

1. Peel avocado. Cut into large quarters.
2. In food processor, place ingredients. Process until creamy.

A&B Dill Dip

1/2 cup mayonnaise
1/2 cup sour cream
2 tablespoons minced fresh dill (or 1 tablespoon dried dill)
2 tablespoons chopped parsley
2 tablespoons chopped scallions
1/2 teaspoon lemon juice or vinegar
1/2 teaspoon salt
1/2 teaspoon black pepper

In a small bowl, combine all ingredients. Stir until well blended. Refrigerate.

A&B Cream Cheese Dip

2 8-ounce packages cream cheese, softened
1 scallion, minced
1 large clove garlic, crushed through a press
1 dash cayenne pepper
1 dash salt
1 dash vinegar or lemon juice
1/2 teaspoon dried dill
1/2 teaspoon dried basil
1/2 teaspoon dried marjoram
1/2 teaspoon dried thyme
1/2 teaspoon dried tarragon

In a medium bowl, combine all ingredients. Stir until well blended. Cover and refrigerate.

A&B Chutney Cheese Spread

1 8-ounce package cream cheese
2 cups shredded sharp cheddar cheese (about 8 ounces)
2 tablespoons dry sherry
1/2 cup mango chutney, chopped
1/4 cup scallions, chopped
1 teaspoon curry powder
1/4 teaspoon salt
Dash hot pepper sauce or cayenne pepper

In a medium bowl combine cream cheese, Cheddar cheese, curry powder, salt, hot sauce, and sherry. Blend until smooth and well blended. Cover and refrigerate until firm, about 2 hours. Top with chutney and sprinkle with scallions.

A&B Horseradish Sauce

1 cup sour cream
1/3 cup horseradish
1 tablespoon fresh lemon juice or vinegar
Pinch white pepper

In a small bowl, combine all ingredients. Stir until well blended. Cover and refrigerate 1 hour.

A&B Blue Cheese Dip

1 cup blue cheese (4 ounces)
1 tablespoon white vinegar
1 scallion, chopped
1/2 cup mayonnaise
1/2 cup sour cream
1 clove garlic, crushed through a press

In a small bowl, combine all ingredients. Stir until well blended. Cover and refrigerate.

Neutral
MENUS

Mediterranean A&B Cabbage Roll

1 large white cabbage
1/2 pound mushrooms, chopped in small pieces
2 celery sticks, chopped
1 cup parsley, chopped
1 cup cilantro, chopped
1/2 cup carrots, grated
3 egg yolks
1/2 cup sour cream
3 large onions, chopped
1 clove garlic, crushed through a press
4 tablespoons butter or olive oil
1 pinch thyme
1 pinch cumin and fennel herbs
1 pinch pepper and 1 pinch sea salt
1 tablespoon sweet Hungarian paprika

1. Place cabbage in a vegetable steamer, for 5–7 minutes (or in boiling water). Cook until leaves are tender when pierced with tip of sharp knife. Separate tender leaves. Chop heart of the cabbage in small pieces, keep it for the stuffing-mixture.

2. In a large frying pan, heat oil, add onions; cook until golden brown. Add mushrooms, celery sticks, parsley, cilantro, small chopped pieces of cabbage, and carrots. Season with sea salt, thyme, cumin, fennel herbs, pepper to taste, cook for 20 minutes, stirring frequently. After 20 minutes, set aside, cover, let cool. Add the egg yolks to the stuffing-mixture. Mix well. Set aside.
3. On a large plate, arrange one or two leaves and form mixture into balls. Arrange mixture on prepared cabbage leaves. Wrap cabbage around mixture. Bind each with string.
4. In a large frying pan, melt 4 tablespoons of olive oil over medium heat. Add cabbage rolls. Cook cabbage rolls, turning, until golden brown.
5. Preheat oven to 300°F. Place rolls on a baking pan. Mix sour cream and 1/2 cup of water. Pour over rolls. Sprinkle Hungarian paprika. Bake it until crispy brown. Serve warm.

Mediterranean Green A&B Peppers

8 green bell peppers
2 middle-size onions, chopped
1/2 pound mushrooms, chopped in small pieces
2 celery sticks, chopped
1 cup parsley, chopped
1 cup cilantro, chopped
1/2 cup carrots, grated
3 egg yolks
1/2 cup sour cream
2 large onions, chopped
1 clove garlic, crushed through the press
4 tablespoon butter or olive oil
1 pinch thyme
1 pinch cumin
1 pinch fennel herb
1 pinch black pepper
1 pinch sea salt
1 tablespoon sweet Hungarian paprika

1. With a sharp knife, cut off green pepper tops. Carefully remove seeds and veins, leaving stems intact.

2. In a large frying pan, heat oil, add onion, cook until golden brown. Add mushrooms, celery sticks, parsley, cilantro, carrots. Season with sea salt, thyme, cumin, fennel herb, black pepper to taste. Cook for 20 minutes, stirring frequently. After 20 minutes, set aside, cover, let cool.
3. Add egg yolks to the stuffing mixture, mix well, set aside.
4. In a large frying pan, heat oil over medium heat.
5. Stuff peppers with mixture. Fry peppers until golden brown.
6. Place peppers in a baking pan.
7. Mix sour cream and water, pour over peppers, sprinkle sweet Hungarian paprika, bake it for further 30 minutes until crispy brown. Serve warm.

Classic A&B Ratatouille

1 medium eggplant
6 zucchini
1 yellow bell pepper, core, seed and coarsely dice
1 green bell pepper, core, seed and coarsely dice
1 red bell pepper, core, seed and coarsely dice
1 tablespoon olive oil
2 onions, sliced
1 clove garlic, crushed through a press
Sea salt to taste
Pepper to taste
1/2 vegetable or chicken broth (can or cubes)
1/2 tablespoon thyme leaves
1/2 tablespoon rosemary
1 tablespoon fresh parsley, chopped

1. Fry briefly onions, garlic in olive oil. Add other prepared vegetables and fry briefly until lightly browned. Season with sea salt and pepper.
2. Add broth. Stir in thyme leaves and rosemary.
3. Cover and cook over low heat until tender.
4. Sprinkle with parsley. Serve warm. (You can eat it either as Neutral, or as A with bread, rice or potato, or B poultry or meat).

A&B Ratatouille Normandy

1 can (15 1/2-ounce) garbanzo beans, drained
2 cups eggplants, diced
2 cups zucchini, sliced
1-1/2 cups onion, sliced
1 cup red bell pepper, sliced
1/2 cup celery, sliced
2 teaspoons olive oil
1 tablespoon sweet Hungarian paprika
2 teaspoons dried oregano
2 teaspoons dried basil
1/2 teaspoon red pepper, crushed
1/2 bunch cilantro, chopped
1/2 bunch parsley, chopped
1 cup mozzarella, grated
1 cup feta cheese, crumbled

1. In a large pan, spread diced eggplants. Sprinkle sea salt evenly. Let stand for 1 hour.
2. In a fry pan, heat oil, and fry eggplants until golden brown.
3. Remove eggplants from pan and spread over kitchen paper.

4. In the fry pan, reduce oil to a maximum 1 cup. Add onion, fry until golden brown. Add zucchini, peppers, celery, parsley, cilantro, and oregano. Turn them quickly around, and add eggplants and garbanzo beans.
5. Place all of that in a baking pan.
6. Preheat the oven to 350°F.
7. Mix mozzarella and feta cheese; sprinkle over the mixture.
8. Put the baking pan in the preheated oven for 30 minutes. Serve warm.

A&B Terrine d' Alsace

12 oz. cauliflower
11 oz. broccoli
1-1/2 teaspoon butter or olive oil
1 cup cream
1 cup cream diluted with filtered water
4 egg yolks
1/4 cup almonds, toasted, grated
Sea salt
Freshly ground pepper
Nutmeg

1. Preheat oven to 350°F.
2. Trim the cauliflower into florets. In a large saucepan, cook cream for 8 to 10 minutes. Remove cauliflower and reserve sauce. Remove hard stalks from the florets, return them to the cooking sauce, cook until tender.
3. Puree the cauliflower stalks along with the sauce. Add nutmeg, sea salt and pepper to taste.
4. In a hand blender, puree cauliflower, cream and cream diluted with milk through a strainer.

5. Beat together the cauliflower mixture and the egg yolks.
6. Line a loaf pan or terrine with aluminum foil and grease with butter or olive oil and fill with the cauliflower and broccoli florets.
7. Cover the broccoli and cauliflower mixture with the sauce, and seal the loaf pan or terrine by folding the aluminum foil.
8. Put hot water in a baking pan. Bake in the preheated oven for 40 minutes.
9. Garnish the finished terrine or loaf pan with the roasted, grated almonds. Cut into slices. Serve warm.

A&B Ramses Beans
with the A&B Ramses Salad

2 pounds small fava beans
1 pound skinless fava beans
1 pound garbanzo beans (chickpeas)
1/2 pound yellow lentils
1 large garlic bulb, crushed through a press
2 tablespoon cumin
2 tablespoon dried coriander
Salt to taste
Pepper to taste

1. Wash beans and lentils separately. In a big bowl, combine fava beans, skinless fava beans, and garbanzo beans. Cover beans with plenty of (distilled) cold water. <u>Soak beans for 3–4 hours, or longer for better results</u>. Remove from water.
2. In a large saucepan, bring water to a boil. Add fava beans and garbanzo beans. Cover with water, 4 inches above. Reduce heat
3. Check the water level every hour; <u>exchange water</u> and add water if necessary.

4. Simmer over medium-low heat for 4–5 hours, until soft. As soon as beans are soft, add lentils. Let cook, for 1 hour, until soft. Add garlic, cumin, coriander, salt, and pepper. Let stand, for 30 minutes. Serve warm; top the A&B Ramses Beans with A&B Ramses Salad. OPTIONAL: mash beans with mixer. Top beans with A&B Ramses Salad.

TIP: Leftovers stored in small single serving bowls or plastic bags can be frozen for later consumption.

A&B Ramses Salad

5–6 fresh hot peppers, such as jalapenos
2–3 large tomatoes
2 large onions
1 head lettuce
1 bunch cilantro
6 large cloves garlic
1 tablespoon coriander
1 tablespoon cumin
Salt to taste
Pepper to taste
1/2 cup vinegar
1/2 cup olive oil

Combine all ingredients in a food processor. Process until well blended to form a pulp. Top A&B Ramses Beans with 3 tablespoons A&B Ramses Salad.

TIP: Place any remaining A&B Ramses Salad in a container and cover with olive oil 2 inches above pulp. Refrigerate for later use. Also tastes great with whole wheat bread or pita.

Artichokes "Milano" with Tofu

1 can artichokes
1/2 cup tofu
2 teaspoons olive oil
2 tablespoons fresh lemon juice
2 tablespoon apple vinegar
1/2 teaspoon mustard
Sea salt to taste
Pepper to taste

1. Put tofu in a blender or food processor, add oil, fresh lemon juice, mustard and tofu. Blend until smooth. Season with sea salt and pepper to taste.
2. Place artichokes on a large plate.
3. Place tofu mixture on a small plate.

A&B Tofu à la Empress Xia

8 oz tofu
1 eggplant, diced
1 zucchini, diced
1 red bell pepper, diced
1 large onion, minced
1/2 bunch fresh dill, chopped
2 cloves garlic, crushed through the press
1 dried Chile pepper, crumbled
1 tablespoon saffron (or foil packet)
1/2 tablespoon cumin
1/2 cup vegetable bouillon
1-1/2 oz pine nuts
1 tablespoon soy sauce
2 tablespoons soy sauce
1/4 cup olive oil
2 cups (filtered) water
Sea salt to taste
Pepper to taste

1. Cut the tofu into cubes, add soy sauce, set aside.

2. In a saucepan, heat the oil over medium heat. Add onion, garlic, zucchini, eggplant, bell pepper, increase heat, let cook for 4 minutes, while stirring.
3. Add vegetable bouillon and bring to a boil. Add Chile pepper and saffron to the bouillon. Add pine nuts, Chile pepper, currants and (filtered) water. Season with sea salt, pepper and cumin to taste.
4. In a skillet, heat olive oil; add tofu and fry until crispy.
5. Sprinkle dill over the tofu. Serve warm.

A&B Broccoli Françoise

2 cups (precut) broccoli florets
1 pound firm tofu, drained and cut into 1/4-inch cubes
3/4 cup (filtered) water
1-1/2 tablespoons minced garlic
2 tablespoons butter
2 tablespoons olive oil
1/2 teaspoon sea salt
2-1/2 teaspoons soy flower
2 tablespoons sesame oil
2 teaspoons fresh lemon juice or apple vinegar
2 tablespoons soy sauce
2 tablespoons teriyaki sauce

1. Mix soy flower, sesame oil, fresh lemon juice or apple vinegar, soy sauce and teriyaki in a small bowl, stirring with a whisk; set aside.
2. In a large skillet, heat olive oil over medium-high heat. Add the tofu, and sprinkle with sea salt. Cook 10 minutes until golden brown, tossing frequently. Remove tofu from pan and keep warm.
3. Add filtered water, broccoli, and garlic to saucepan. Cover and cook 5 minutes until crisp-tender, stirring occasionally.
4. Add soy sauce mixture and tofu, stirring gently to coat. Cook 2 minutes, stirring occasionally.
5. Serve with salad to season.

A&B Spaghetti Squash "Renato",

3 cups spaghetti squash
1 can (15.5 ounce) garbanzo beans, drained
1 cup cucumber, diced
2 cups tomatoes, chipped
1/4 cup green bell pepper, diced
1/4 cup red onion, diced
1/2 cup feta crumbled feta cheese
2 tablespoon pitted olives, chopped
2 teaspoons olive oil
3 tablespoons apple vinegar
2 garlic cloves, crushed through a press
1 teaspoon dried oregano
1/4 teaspoon sea salt
1/4 teaspoon black pepper

1. In a large bowl, mix olive oil, apple vinegar, garlic, oregano, sea salt and pepper, stir well with a whisk.
2. Cook spaghetti squash.
3. In a large bowl, combine spaghetti squash and remaining ingredients, add mixture; toss well. Cover and chill.
4. Serve immediately.

A&B Beans à la Bretagne

1 can (28-ounce) white beans
1 can (16 ounce) garbanzo beans, rinsed and drained
1 can (19-ounce) black beans, rinsed and drained
1 can (15-ounce) lima beans, rinsed and drained
1 can (15.5-ounce) kidney beans, rinsed and drained
1/2 cup (filtered) water
1/4 cup apple vinegar
1 large onion, diced

1. In a large skillet, heat olive oil over medium heat, add onion, and cook until golden brown.
2. Preheat oven to 350°F.
3. Grease large baking dish.
4. Mix onions and beans, water and apple vinegar, place on baking dish and cover.
5. Bake for 1 hour; uncover and bake 25 more minutes.
6. Serve warm.

A&B Mushrooms St. Tropez

1/2 pound mushrooms
1 tablespoon butter
1 tablespoon fresh lemon juice
Dash sea salt
Dash garlic salt
Soy sauce
4-6 egg yolks
1 bunch parsley, chopped

1. Wash mushrooms; cut ends from stems. Cut mushrooms into slices.
2. In a saucepan, melt butter. Add mushrooms, tossing lightly in butter, until soft. Add soy sauce.
3. In a bowl, beat egg yolks. Pour over mushrooms. Cook for 4 minutes. Season to taste.
4. Sprinkle fresh parsley over mushrooms.
5. Serve with rice salad.

A&B Ragout "Michelle"

1 can (19-ounce) garbanzo beans, drained
3 cups butternut squash, diced
6 Portobello Mushrooms, sliced
1-1/2 cups parsnip, sliced
2 cups leeks, sliced
1-1/2 cups carrots, sliced
1 cup celery, sliced
12 cloves of garlic, cut in half
5 teaspoons olive oil
1 tablespoon soy flour
2 bay leaves
2 thyme sprigs
1/2 cup fresh parsley, chopped
1/2 cup heavy cream
1 tablespoon soy flour
1 cup dry red wine
1/2 cup bouillon
3/4 teaspoon sea salt
1/2 teaspoon black pepper

1. In a pan, heat olive oil over medium heat. Add squash, parsnips, leeks, carrots, celery and cloves, and sauté for 8–10 minutes until golden brown, stirring frequently.
2. Add bay leaves, thyme. Stir in heavy cream, soy flour and wine. Lower heat, and cook for 5 minutes.
3. Stir in the broth and garbanzos. Cover and simmer for 20 minutes, until tender. Stir in 1/2 teaspoon salt, pepper and parsley. Remove bay leaves.
4. In a large skillet, heat oil over medium heat. Add mushrooms and cook for 5 minutes, while stirring. Sprinkle with 1/4 teaspoon se salt.
5. Pour ragout over mushrooms. Serve warm.

Spicy New Yorker A&B Mushrooms

4 cups mixed mushrooms, sliced (Portobello, shiitake, etc.)
1 middle sized onion, chopped
1-1/2 tablespoons olive oil
2-3 cloves garlic, crushed through the press
6 oz. goat's cheese
1 tablespoon Chile oil
Sea salt to taste
Pepper to taste
Thyme to taste

1. Preheat oven to 400°F.
2. In a saucepan, heat oil, add onions. Cook until golden brown.
3. Combine mushrooms with olive oil, garlic, salt and pepper.
4. Place mixture in a baking dish. Bake for 20 minutes.
5. Sprinkle goat cheese over mushrooms.
6. Sprinkle with Chile oil, pepper and thyme. Serve warm.

White A&B Beans "Miami"

2 cans (15-ounce) white beans, drained
1 cup onions, chopped
1/2 cup fresh parsley, minced
1 tablespoon dried rosemary
1 teaspoon lemon rind, grated
1/2 cup (filtered) water
1 cup white wine
1/2 teaspoon black pepper
1 bacon slices, cut in cubes

1. In a large skillet, cook bacon over medium heat until crisp.
2. In a saucepan, combine beans, water, lemon rind, wine and pepper.
3. Simmer for 30 minutes.
4. Sprinkle (uncooked) bacon cubes and parsley over beans. Serve warm with salad.

A&B Vegetables Parisian

6 carrots, cut into cubes
2 medium zucchini, sliced
2 medium yellow squash
2 tablespoons butter
2 teaspoons fresh lemon juice or vinegar
Soy sauce to taste
Seasoning to taste

In a vegetable steamer, place carrots over boiling water for 10 minutes. Add zucchini and steam until tender, for 7 minutes. Arrange vegetables on a plate. Cut squash in cubes. Combine butter and lemon juice (or vinegar) and pour over vegetables. Season to taste.

A&B Soufflé Côte d' Azur

1 large cauliflower, cored and broken into small florets
3 tablespoons olive oil
2 egg yolks
1/4 cup parsley, chopped
1 pinch sweet Hungarian paprika or other paprika
1 pinch nutmeg

1. Preheat oven to 350°F.
2. In a saucepan, cook cauliflower in boiling salted water until just tender, for 10 minutes. Remove from heat.
3. In a small soufflé dish, heat 1 tablespoon oil.
4. Whisk two egg yolks, with 2 teaspoons oil, nutmeg, pepper, and parsley.
5. Transfer cauliflower to soufflé dish
6. Spread mixture over cauliflower. Place in a broiler until soufflé is golden brown, 5–7 minutes.

La A&B Aubergine
in Cocoscreme Sauce

2 large eggplants
1 can cocos milk
1/4 pound butter
1-1/2 cup vegetable or corn oil
2 red bell pepper, chopped in cubes
1 middle onion, chopped
1 lemon, pressed

1. With a sharp knife, remove stem end of eggplant. Cut eggplants in 1/2-inch slices.
2. On a large plate, place eggplants, sprinkle with sea salt, let stand for one hour (to help the extract the water of the eggplants).
3. In a large saucepan, heat butter, add onion and fry until brown. Add pepper, simmer for 20 minutes. Add cocos milk, bring it to a boil. Cover and set aside.
4. In a large fry pan, heat vegetable or corn oil over medium heat. Fry eggplants until golden brown on both sides.

5. Remove eggplants from pan. Place it on kitchen paper until oil is absorbed by paper. Place it on a decorative plate.
6. Heat the saucepan with the pepper again, pour it over eggplants.
7. Pour lemon over eggplants and pepper. Serve warm.

A&B Cabbage Budapest

1 white cabbage, sliced
1 pound onions, diced
2 cups vegetable water (or bouillon cube)
Butter to taste
2 cups heavy cream
1 cup sour cream
2 tablespoons butter
Sea salt to taste
2 teaspoons Hungarian paprika
Soy sauce to taste

1. In a large saucepan, cook onions in butter until golden brown. Add vegetable water and sea salt to taste.
2. Place cabbage in saucepan and cook for 15–20 minutes. Remove from heat and drain.
3. Combine heavy cream and sour cream with paprika and season to taste. Sprinkle mixture over cabbage. Let stand 10 minutes.

Neutral

Desserts

Creamy A&B Walnut Dessert

1 cup cottage cheese (or Ricotta cheese)
1/2 cup heavy cream, whipped
2 egg yolks (*)
1/8 cup walnuts

In a medium bowl, combine ingredients. Mix well.
Refrigerate.

Creamy A&B Blueberry Dessert

2 pounds blueberries
2 cups heavy cream, whipped
Sweetener

Mix ingredients well. Refrigerate.

(*) There is some danger of salmonella from uncooked egg yolks.

Neutral
Ice Cream

A&B Vanilla Ice Cream

2 cups heavy cream, whipped
4 egg yolks (*)
1 teaspoon vanilla
1 cup chopped walnuts
Artificial sweetener

1. In a processor, combine whipped cream with egg yolks, vanilla, and artificial sweetener. Process until mixture is foaming.
2. Put mixture into a plastic bowl. Put in freezer. Chill at least 1 to 1-1/2 hours. Serve with whipped cream. Garnish with walnuts.

(*) There is some danger of salmonella from uncooked egg yolks.

A&B Hazelnut Ice Cream

2 cups heavy cream, whipped
4 egg yolks (*)
2 cups hazelnuts, crushed
2 packets artificial sweetener

1. In a processor, combine whipped cream with egg yolks, hazelnuts, and artificial sweetener. Process until mixture is foaming.
2. Put mixture into plastic bowl. Put in freezer. Chill at least 1 to 1-1/2 hours. Serve with whipped cream. Garnish with hazelnuts.

(*) *There is some danger of salmonella from uncooked egg yolks.*

"A"

A
Soups

Classic A&B Potato Soup

8 potatoes (medium to large), chopped in cubes
6–7 cups (distilled) water
2 tablespoons butter
1 teaspoon olive oil
1 large onion, chopped
1 clove garlic, minced
2 cups celery, chopped
4 cups vegetable bouillon
  (OPTIONAL: 4 bouillon cubes)
 teaspoon dried tarragon
1/4 teaspoon dried sage
1 teaspoon dried thyme
1 dash cayenne pepper
1 dash nutmeg
1 dash sea salt

In a large saucepan, melt butter and heat oil. Add onion, garlic, celery, potatoes, bouillon, and spices. Add bouillon to cover vegetables. Bring to a boil. Simmer until vegetables are soft, for 20 minutes. Mash vegetables and potatoes. Serve warm.

A&B Corn Soup

2 fresh ears of corn (or one 10-ounce package frozen whole kernel corn, thawed)
1/4 cup onion, chopped
1 clove garlic, minced
1 tablespoon butter
1 cup chicken broth (or bouillon cube)
Bottled hot sauce to taste
1/2 cup heavy cream
1/2 cup sour cream
1/4 teaspoon sea salt
1/8 teaspoon pepper
Cilantro, chopped
Parsley, chopped

1. If using fresh corn, use a sharp knife to cut off just the kernel tips. Then scrape the cob with a knife.
2. In a blender container or food processor combine half of the corn, sour cream, and heavy cream. Cover and blend or process until smooth, stopping machine occasionally to scrape down sides. Set mixture aside.
3. In a medium saucepan, cook onion and garlic in butter until tender but not brown. Stir in mixture, remaining corn, broth, salt, pepper, and hot pepper sauce. Bring to boiling. Reduce heat and simmer for 20–25 minutes. Gradually stir in cream. Heat through, but do not boil. Season to taste. Garnish with parsley and cilantro.

A
MENUS

A&B Mushroom Soufflé

1–1/2 cups whole rye flour or 1/2 cup whole wheat flour
1/2 pound butter
1/2 cup (filtered) water
1 pound mushrooms, sliced
1 small onion, chopped
1 egg yolk
1 cup heavy cream
Sea salt to taste
Black pepper to taste

1. In a medium mixing bowl, combine whole rye flour or whole wheat flour, butter, sea salt, and 1/2 cup (filtered) water. Stir mixture with your hands.
2. Preheat oven to 350°F. Brush soufflé pan with butter before placing 2/3 of the dough on baking sheet. Reserve 1/3 of the dough; set aside.
3. In a small saucepan, fry chopped onions. Add mushrooms, egg yolks, heavy cream, and spices. Let cook for 10 minutes.
4. Place mixture on dough. Cover soufflé with remaining dough. Bake until brown and crispy.

A&B Crêpe d' Amoureuse

2 cups (filtered and warm) water
1 cup wheat flour
1 cup chickpea flour
1/2 teaspoon sea salt
2 tablespoons olive oil
Butter
4 cups vegetable bouillon (broth of cube)
1/2 ounce dried mushrooms
1/2 cup (filtered) water
2 tablespoons olive oil
3/4 cup red wine
2 tablespoons honey
2 cups onions, chopped
8-ounces shiitake mushroom caps, coarsely chopped
8-ounce mushrooms, coarsely chopped
1/2 teaspoon ground black pepper
1/4 teaspoon nutmeg
1/4 teaspoon sea salt
6 cloves garlic, minced
1/4 cup fresh parsley, finely chopped
2 teaspoons soy flour
2 tablespoons (filtered) water

1. In a bowl, combine wheat flour, chickpea flour and 1/2 teaspoon sea salt. Add 2 cups of (filtered) warm water and olive oil, stirring with a whisk until smooth; let stand for 20 minutes.
2. In a skillet or crêpe pan, coated with butter over medium heat. Remove skillet or pan from heat. Pour 1/2 cup liquid dough into pan; quickly shake pan in all directions so (liquid) dough covers pan with a thin film. Cook about 40 seconds.
3. Carefully lift edge of crêpe with spatula to test if it's done.
4. Turn crêpe as soon as it can be shaken loose from the pan and when one side is lightly browned. Cook 30 seconds on each side.
5. Place crêpe on a towel; cool until you can handle. Repeat procedure until you made 12 crêpes. Stack crêpes between single layers of wax paper to prevent sticking.
6. In a medium sauce pan, bring bouillon and 1/2 cup (filtered) water to a boil. Remove from heat, stir in mushrooms. Set aside for 30 minutes.
7. Strain mixture through a sieve and put it into a bowl. Reserve bouillon and mushrooms. Add honey and red wine; set aside.
8. In a large skillet, heat 2 tablespoons olive oil over medium heat, add onion; sauté for 3 minutes. Add reserved mushrooms; sauté 1 minute.
9. Add button and shiitake mushrooms. Cook for 4 minutes until mushrooms release moisture, stirring occasionally.

10. Reduce heat to medium, add nutmeg, pepper, garlic and salt to taste. Cook 1 minute, stirring frequently; add 3/4 cup bouillon mixture, reduce heat and simmer for 15 minutes, stirring occasionally.
11. Bring remaining bouillon mixture to a boil, cook about 10–12 minutes. Mix 2 tablespoons (filtered) water with soy flour, stirring with a whisk. Stir cornstarch mixture into bouillon mixture, bring to a boil. Cook for 2 minutes, until thickens.
12. Put 1/3 cup mushroom mixture in center of each crêpe. Fold sides and ends over, and place, seam side down, on a plate. Repeat procedure with remaining mushroom mixture and crêpes. Top each serving with about 1/4 cup sauce; sprinkle with 2 teaspoons parsley. Serve warm.

Venetian A&B Polenta

1 cup polenta (instant dry)
4 cups (filtered) water
1 tablespoon olive oil
1 tablespoon butter
1 large onion, chopped
2 tablespoons minced garlic
2 cans (15-ounce) garbanzo beans
1/4 cup fresh lemon juice
1 teaspoon cumin
1/4 teaspoon pepper
1 cup crème fraîche
3/4 cup sour crème
1/2 cup scallion
1 teaspoon dried oregano

1. In a medium saucepan, bring water to a boil. Add polenta, gradually, stirring constantly with a whisk. Reduce heat, simmer for 3 minutes, stirring constantly.
2. Remove from heat, stir in butter, cover and set aside.
3. In a large skillet, heat oil over medium heat. Add onion and garlic, sauté for 3 minutes. Add garbanzo beans, pepper, cumin, crème fraîche and fresh lemon juice, bring to a boil. Reduce heat after boiling. Simmer for 6 minutes and stir in scallions.
4. Place polenta on a decorative plate. Pour mixture over polenta, top with sour cream. Serve warm.

American Stuffed A&B Peppers

2 red bell peppers
2 yellow bell peppers
2 green bell peppers
2 middle-size onions, chopped
1/2 pound mushrooms, chopped in small pieces
2 celery sticks, chopped
1 cup parsley, chopped
1/2 cup carrots, grated
3 egg yolks
1/2 cup sour cream
2 large onions, chopped
1 clove garlic, crushed through the press
4 tablespoons butter or olive oil
1 pinch thyme
1 pinch cumin
1 pinch fennel herb
1 pinch black pepper
1 pinch sea salt
1 tablespoon sweet Hungarian paprika

1. With a sharp knife, cut off green pepper tops. Carefully remove seeds and veins, leaving stems intact.
2. In a large frying pan, heat oil, add onion; cook until golden brown. Add mushrooms, celery sticks, parsley, cilantro and carrots. Season with sea salt, thyme cumin, fennel, herb, black pepper to taste. Cook for 20 minutes, stirring frequently. After 20 minutes, set aside, cover, let cool.
3. Add egg yolks to the stuffing mixture, mix well, set aside.
4. In a large frying pan, heat oil over medium heat.
5. Stuff peppers with mixture. Fry peppers until golden brown.
6. Place peppers in a baking pan.
7. Mix sour cream and water, pour over peppers, sprinkle sweet Hungarian paprika, bake it for further 30 minutes until crispy brown.
8. Serve with potatoes, rice (see recipe), couscous or bread.

Traditional A&B Beans

1 can (28-ounce) beans
1 small onion, diced
1/4 cup sorghum
1/4 cup white or brown sugar
1 teaspoon teriyaki sauce
1 teaspoon mustard

1. Preheat oven to 350°F.
2. In a baking dish, put olive oil or butter. Add beans and onion, sorghum, mustard, sugar and Teriyaki sauce. Stir together.
3. Bake for 45 minutes. Serve warm with salad.

A
Pasta

A&B Lasagna

1 packet lasagna, preferable whole wheat
1 pound mushrooms, sliced thinly
1/2 bunch celery sticks, finely chopped
2 medium carrots, chopped
1/2 bunch parsley, chopped
1/2 bunch cilantro, chopped
2 large onions, sliced
1 tablespoon dried oregano
1 teaspoon garlic powder, or fresh minced garlic
1/2 cup olive oil
Sea salt to taste
Pepper to taste
2 tablespoons Teriyaki Sauce
4 tablespoons Ricotta cheese
1 cup heavy cream
1/2 cup feta cheese, crumbled
2 cups mozzarella, grated

1. In a stockpot, bring water to a boil, add a teaspoon sea salt, 2 tablespoon olive oil, add lasagna and let cook until dente. Set aside.

2. In a large fry pan or wok, heat olive oil over medium heat. Add onions, cook until golden brown, stirring frequently.
3. Add celery, garlic and carrots, stir for 3 – 5 minutes. Add cilantro and parsley, mix it well, and cook for another 3 minutes. Add 1 large tablespoon Ricotta cheese with 1/4 cup of heavy cream. Mix it well and add oregano, Teriyaki sauce, sea salt and pepper to taste.
4. In a lasagna pan, place lasagna evenly. Spread 1/3 of the vegetable mixture evenly over the lasagna.
5. Take another layer of lasagna, cover the mixture, spread another 1/3 of the vegetable mixture and cover the lasagna.
6. Take another layer of lasagna and spread the last third of the mixture over the lasagna.
7. Cover the vegetable mixture with the remaining lasagna. Let stand.
8. Mix the Ricotta cheese and heavy cream, mix it well and pour it over the lasagna.
9. Mix mozzarella cheese with feta cheese, mix it well and spread it over the lasagna.
10. Preheat oven to 300°F.
11. Put lasagna pan in the oven, and bake until golden browned. Serve it hot.

Tip: You can freeze all leftovers.

A&B Lasagna Côte d' Azur

1 package lasagna, preferably whole wheat
2 middle-sized eggplants, chopped in cubes
1/2 pound mushrooms, sliced
1/2 bunch of celery sticks, finely chopped
2 medium carrots, chopped
1/2 bunch of parsley, chopped
1/2 bunch of cilantro, chopped
2 large onions, sliced
1/2 tablespoon dried oregano
1 tablespoon garlic powder, or fresh minced garlic
1/2 cup olive oil
3 cup vegetable oil
Sea salt to taste
Pepper to taste
2 tablespoons Teriyaki sauce
4 tablespoons Ricotta cheese
1 cup heavy cream
1/2 cup feta cheese, crumbled
2 cups mozzarella, grated

1. Spread eggplant cubes over kitchen paper, and sprinkle them with sea salt. Let stand for at least 1-1/2 hours (to lose a lot of water).
2. In a large frying pan or wok, heat vegetable oil, add eggplants, let cook until golden brown.

3. Remove from wok and spread over kitchen paper (to soak the oil).
4. In a stockpot, bring water to a boil; add 1 teaspoon sea salt and 2 tablespoons olive oil. Add lasagna and let cook until dente. Set aside.
5. In a large frying pan or wok, remove oil and replace it with olive oil. Heat it over high heat until the oil is real hot, add onions, cook until golden brown. Add celery, carrots, parsley and cilantro, stir frequently very well for 10 minutes. Add mushrooms, mix it well. Cook for further 3 – 5 minutes.
6. Add garlic, oregano and 1/2 cup heavy cream and 2 tablespoons Ricotta cheese. Mix well, stir frequently for 1 minute, add Teriyaki sauce. Remove from heat, add eggplants. Set aside.
7. In a lasagna pan, place lasagna evenly, spread 1/3 of the eggplants mixture evenly over the lasagna.
8. Take another layer of lasagna, cover the mixture, and spread 1/3 of the eggplant mixture and cover the lasagna.
9. Take another layer of lasagna, spread 1/3 of the eggplants mixture over the lasagna.
10. Take another layer of lasagna, spread 1/3 of the eggplants mixture over the lasagna

11. Cover the lasagna mixture with the remaining lasagna. Let stand.
12. Mix Ricotta cheese and heavy cream. Mix it well and pour it over lasagna.
13. Mix mozzarella cheese and feta cheese, and spread over lasagna.
14. Preheat oven to 300°F.
15. Put lasagna pan in oven and bake until golden brown. Serve it hot.

Bavarian A&B "Knoedel" with Chanterelle In Crème Sauce

KNOEDEL (dumplings)
5 bagels, preferably whole wheat (must be at least 2 days old, cut in 1/4 inches)
5 rolls (must be at least two days old, cut in 1/4 inch slices)
1 cup hot (filtered)water
1 cup heavy cream
1 bunch parsley, chopped small
1 tablespoon marjoram
1 tablespoon sea salt
1/2 tablespoon black pepper
2 egg yolks
1 small onion, chopped
2 tablespoons olive oil
1 quart butter

CRÈME SAUCE
1/2 pound chanterelle, cut in smaller pieces
1/2 pound mushrooms, sliced
1 large onion, chopped
1 cup heavy cream
1 bunch parsley, chopped
1 tablespoon pepper
1/2 tablespoon sea salt
1 tablespoon butter

1. <u>CRÈME SAUCE</u>: In small saucepan, heat the butter over medium heat and add onions until glassy.
2. Add mushrooms and chanterelle, add 2 tablespoons water, stir frequently for 10 minutes.
3. Add pepper, sea salt and heavy cream. Mix it well with the mushrooms and chanterelle. Turn heat down, let stand over very low heat.
4. <u>KNOEDEL</u>: In a very large bowl, mix bagels and rolls together.
5. In a small saucepan, mix hot water with heavy cream. Bring it to a boil.
6. Add water and heavy cream mixture to bagel and rolls. Cover and let stand for 10 minutes.
7. In a small saucepan, heat butter over medium heat butter, add onions, stir frequently, let cook until golden brown.
8. Mix all ingredients above mentioned with the onions. Pour it over the bagels and rolls.
9. Mix it well and knead the mixture with your hand until the mixture is smooth, ready to be formed into Knoedel (dumplings). In case the mixture had become too soft, add bread crumbs.
10. In a large stockpot (70% filled), bring (filtered) water to a boil, add formed Knoedel (one after the other). Keep it boiling for 10 minutes. With a large spoon, take the Knoedel out.
11. In a large bowl, place the Knoedel. Pour the Crème Sauce evenly over the Knoedel. Sprinkle parsley evenly. Serve warm.

A&B Summer Pasta
with Fresh Tomato Sauce

1/2 pound Farfalla (or any other pasta)
1/2 pound plum or cherry tomatoes, coarsely chopped into
small pieces.
4 tablespoon olive oil
1 bunch fresh basil, chopped into small pieces
1 tablespoon oregano
2 garlic clove, crushed through the press
Sea salt
Pepper

1. Chop tomatoes into small pieces; keep the juice of the tomatoes. Add chopped basil, add all other ingredients, including seasoning, and mix it nicely. And leave it for about 30 minutes in a large bowl.
2. In a stockpot, cook pasta until dente, drain the water.
3. Put the pasta in a large bowl. Add tomato and basil mixture. Serve it immediately.

A&B Orchetta
with Broccoli and Almonds

1 pound Orchetta noodles
1 pound broccoli florets
4 tablespoon olive oil
Sea salt
Pepper to taste
1 cup almonds, thinly sliced

1. In a steam pot (or in a saucepan with salt water) steam or cook broccolis for 3 minutes. Remove broccoli immediately after 3 minutes, and put it in prepared ice water for 3 minutes (so that broccoli will keep their color).
2. Put broccoli in a large strainer, make sure that broccoli are broken into smaller pieces.
3. Cook pasta in very salty water until dente. Drain in strainer.
4. Add broccoli to pasta. Add olive oil, sea salt and pepper to taste. Mix them well together.
5. In a small fry pan, heat two tablespoon butter over medium heat, add almonds, roast until golden brown.
6. On a large plate, place broccoli and pasta and sprinkle almonds evenly over pasta and broccoli. Serve warm.

A&B Macaroni del Forno

1/2 pound macaroni
1 large onion, chopped
1/2 red bell pepper, chopped
1/2 green bell pepper, chopped
10 green olives without pit
2 garlic cloves, crushed through the press
1/2 pound mushrooms, chopped
4 tablespoon olive oil
1 teaspoon dried oregano
1 cup sour cream
1/2 cup crème fraîche
1 cup heavy cream
2 egg yolk
1/2 cup feta cheese, crumbled
Butter
1/2 cup breadcrumbs

1. In a saucepan, cook pasta al dente. Drain it in a sieve.
2. Preheat oven to 200°F.
3. In a baking pan, grease with butter, sprinkle breadcrumbs evenly, set aside.

4. In a fry pan, heat olive oil over medium heat, add onion and garlic until lightly browned. Add peppers, simmer for 10 minutes. Add olives and mushrooms. Season with sea salt and oregano to taste. Simmer for further 5 minutes. Remove from heat, set aside and let cool.
5. Put half of the macaroni in the baking pan, spread the vegetable mixture evenly over macaroni. Add the other half of macaroni and spread it evenly.
6. Mix together sour cream, crème fraîche, egg yolks and feta cheese. Mix well and pour it over the macaroni.
7. Put baking pan in the preheated oven for 30 minutes until crispy brown. Serve it warm.

A&B Spaghetti with Pesto, Basil & Lettuce

1 bunch fresh basil, cut in fine stripes
2 tablespoons pine nuts
2 cloves garlic, crushed through a press
1/2 cup feta cheese, grated
1 cup olive oil
1/2 pound whole wheat spaghetti
1 pinch of sea salt

1. In a fry pan, roast the pine nuts until lightly brown. Set aside, let cool.
2. In a hand blender, add pine nuts, basil, garlic and sea salt. Blend well until puree.
3. Add slowly oil and feta cheese to the puree. Mix it very well.
4. Cook spaghetti al dente. Let drain through a sieve.
5. In a salad bowl, prepare lettuce. Add oil, vinegar and sour cream.
6. On a large plate, place spaghetti and pour Pesto mixture over it. Serve immediately.

Pasta with A&B White Sauce

It would be best for your health to buy pasta made from whole wheat flour. However, if you are healthy to start, you can eat white flour from time to time. Pasta should be served with mixed salads and/or may be eaten with bananas, grapes, fresh figs, fresh dates, dried apples, dried plums, dried figs, dried dates, raisins, and all kind of nuts including peanut). Beer, whiskey, rye and gin are also compatible.

The A&B White Sauce is a basic sauce
that can be used with every pasta dish.

A&B White Sauce

Basic Recipe

6 tablespoons butter
4 tablespoons whole wheat flour
1 cup heavy cream (diluted with 2 cups water)
Pinch of sea salt and freshly ground pepper
Pinch of grated nutmeg, optional

In a saucepan, melt butter over low heat. Slowly add flour a butter melts; stir until smooth. Pour in cream, stirring constantly for 15 minutes or until smooth and velvety. Increase heat and stir until sauce comes to a boil. Low simmer for 10 minutes more, stirring occasionally. Add salt, pepper, and nutmeg to taste. Whisk again until the sauce is smooth.

A&B Rigatoni with Broccoli

1 pound rigatoni
1 bunch fresh broccoli, washed and stems cut off
1/2 cup chopped olives, black and green
1/2 pound fatty bacon, chopped
3 cloves garlic, minced or pressed
1/4 cup dry white wine
7-oz can chicken broth (or 1 cup bouillon)
2 tablespoons butter
1/2 cup fresh Italian parsley, chopped
1 tablespoon basil
1/2 cup olive oil
1 cup A&B White Sauce

1. Prepare A&B White Sauce; set aside.
2. In a saucepan, lightly brown oil, garlic, and bacon for 10 minutes. Add wine and let simmer over medium heat for 5 minutes. Add broken-up broccoli, salt, and pepper to taste; let cook for 10 minutes. Add chicken broth and 1 cup A&B White Sauce; simmer for 5 minutes. Add olives, basil, parsley, and butter; simmer another 3 minutes.
3. While sauce is simmering, cook pasta in boiling salted water until tender but firm. Remove from heat and drain. Place in warm bowl and mix with broccoli sauce. Serve immediately.

A&B Rigatoni à la Gondola

1 pound rigatoni
5 pieces dried mushrooms
1 cup heavy cream
1/2 cup feta cheese, shredded
Fresh oregano to taste
Fresh basil to taste
3 cloves garlic, crushed through a press
1/4 cup olive oil
Olives, chopped (quantity to taste)

1. In a food processor, crush mushrooms; set aside.
2. In a frying pan, cook olive oil; add garlic, oregano, basil, and heavy cream (2 minutes.) Add feta cheese; set aside.
3. In a large saucepan, cook rigatoni in boiling salted water until tender but firm. Remove from heat and drain. Pour mixture over rigatoni. Mix well. Sprinkle crushed mushrooms together with chopped olives over rigatoni.

A&B Spaghetti à la Toscana

1/2 pound spaghetti
4 onions, chopped
2 large cloves garlic, crushed through a press
1-1/2 pounds mushrooms, sliced
2 tablespoons butter
1/2 pound grated fresh cheese (above 60% fat)
1 cup heavy cream
1 teaspoon fresh basil, chopped
1 pinch sea salt
1 pinch pepper
1 teaspoon basil
1 teaspoon oregano

1. In a medium saucepan, cook onions and mushrooms in butter until softened but not brown. Add garlic, salt, and pepper to taste. Add fresh cheese. Cook until melted. Add cream. Mix well; set aside.
2. In a large saucepan, cook pasta in boiling salted water until tender but firm. Remove from heat and drain. Sprinkle mixture over spaghetti. Drizzle fresh basil and oregano to taste.

A&B Fettuccine Alfredo

1 pound fettucine
8 tablespoons butter, softened
1/4 cup heavy cream
1 cup grated mozzarella cheese
Freshly ground pepper

1. Cook pasta in boiling salted water until tender but firm. Remove from heat and drain.
2. Place fettuccine in a warm bowl or on a serving platter. Add butter, cream, and half the mozzarella cheese. Toss fettuccine noodles gently until they are evenly coated. Serve immediately, topped with pepper and remaining mozzarella cheese.

A&B Spaghetti à la Bell Paese

1/2 pound spaghetti
2 large tomatoes
1 bundle fresh basil
Parsley to taste
3 sticks celery
4 cloves garlic, crushed through a press
2 fresh green onions
1/2 tablespoon fresh oregano
Olive oil
Sea salt to taste
Pepper to taste
Seasoning to taste

1. Cut all vegetables in very small pieces (don't cook). Add lemon and olive oil. Mix well.
2. In a large saucepan, cook spaghetti in boiling salted water until tender but firm. Remove from heat and drain. Spread mixture over spaghetti.

A&B Pasta di Paesano

1/2 pound elbow noodles
Feta cheese (quantity to taste)
1 cup heavy cream
4 cloves garlic, crushed through a press
Fresh mint (quantity to taste), chopped
Fresh spinach (quantity to taste), chopped
Olive oil

1. Combine (uncooked) spinach, mint, feta cheese, cream, olive oil, and garlic; set aside.
2. In a saucepan, cook noodles in boiling salted water until tender but firm. Remove from heat and drain. Add mixture to noodles. Mix well.

A&B Spaghetti with Four Cheeses

1 pound spaghetti
2 oz feta cheese
2 oz cream Gouda cheese
2 oz Gorgonzola (Italian soft blue cheese)
2 oz cottage cheese
1/4 cup butter
Sea salt to taste

1. Dice all cheese, except cottage cheese, into 1/4-inch cubes; place in a bowl; set aside.
2. Cook pasta in boiling salted water until tender but firm. Remove from heat and drain. Place spaghetti back into the same pot and add butter and diced cheese.
3. Simmer over medium heat until cheese is melted. Remove from heat and place in warm bowl. Sprinkle with cottage cheese and serve immediately.

A&B Pasta à la Chinoise

1/2 pound spaghetti
4 carrots, sliced
1-1/2 pounds mushrooms, sliced
4 scallions, sliced
2 stalks celery, sliced
Onion, sliced into rings
2 large cloves garlic, crushed through a press or chopped
Butter to taste (or olive oil)
Soy sauce to taste
Cayenne pepper to taste
Ginger to taste
Sea salt to taste
Pepper to taste

1. In a large saucepan or wok, cook onions until golden brown. Gradually add carrots, mushrooms, celery, scallions, garlic, soy sauce, cayenne pepper, ginger, salt and pepper in butter or olive oil until brown; set aside.
2. In a saucepan, cook pasta in boiling salted water until tender but firm. Remove from heat and drain.
3. Add spaghetti to mixture. Mix well.

A&B Macaroni and Cheese

1/2 pound macaroni
3 cups mozzarella, shredded
4–5 cloves garlic, crushed through a press
1 teaspoon oregano
1 teaspoon thyme

1. In a large saucepan, cook macaroni in boiling salted water until tender but firm. Remove from heat and drain.
2. Combine oregano, thyme, and garlic. Sprinkle mixture over macaroni. Sprinkle mozzarella evenly over the macaroni.
3. Preheat oven to 300°F. Place macaroni in a greased baking dish. Bake until macaroni is nicely brown and crisp, about 20 minutes.

A&B Pasta Parisian

1/2 pound rigatoni (or any other type of pasta)
1 large eggplant
1 cup ricotta cheese (or cottage cheese)
1/2 cup heavy cream (diluted with little water)
1/2 cup olive oil
2 large cloves garlic, crushed through a press
2 carrots, cut into thin strips
2 celery stalks, cut into thin strips
4 onions, chopped
Soy sauce to taste
1 teaspoon oregano
1 teaspoon basil
Cayenne pepper to taste

1. Cut eggplant into 3/4-inch cubes. Put eggplant in a strainer. Sprinkle sufficient salt over eggplant. Let stand until fluid is removed, 45 minutes.
2. In a saucepan, cook pasta in boiling salted water until tender but firm. Remove from heat and drain.
3. In a deep frying pan or wok, cook onions, and garlic in hot oil until brown. Add eggplant. Spice with soy sauce, oregano, basil, and cayenne pepper. Reduce heat; cook, stirring occasionally, at least 1/2 hour. Add ricotta (or cottage) cheese as well as 1/2 cup heavy cream. Add mixture to rigatoni. Mix well.

A&B Angel's Hair with Mushrooms-Capelli d' Angelo

1 pound capelli d'angelo
20 whole button mushrooms, cleaned
1/2 pound butter
Freshly ground pepper
4 tablespoons grated mozzarella

Cook pasta in boiling salted water for 1 minute until tender but firm. Sauté mushrooms in butter for 10 minutes or until soft. Add pepper. In a large, warm bowl, place half mushroom mixture; add capelli d'angelo and toss gently. Sprinkle in mozzarella cheese and toss again. Serve warm with mushrooms and butter sauce spooned over.

A&B Angel's Hair Soufflé-Capelli d'Angelo

1/2 pound capelli d'angelo
4 egg yolks, separated
1/4 cup grated mozzarella
1 cup A&B White Sauce

1. Prepare A&B White Sauce; set aside.
2. Cook pasta in boiling salted water for 1 minute or until tender but firm. Remove from heat and drain. In a mixing bowl, combine egg yolks and mozzarella cheese. Mix until stiff.
3. Mix in capelli d'angelo and blend thoroughly.
4. Pour mixture into a buttered soufflé dish. Bake at 450°F, or until soufflé puffs up. Serve immediately with A&B White Sauce.

A&B Pasta "Decamerone",

1/2 pound rigatoni (or any other type of pasta)
1-1/2 pounds mushrooms, sliced
1 can green peas
2 tablespoons butter
2 cups heavy cream
1 cup cream cheese
4 onions, chopped
2 large cloves garlic, crushed through a press

1. In a medium saucepan, cook onions and mushrooms in butter until softened but not brown. Add peas (without fluid), garlic, salt, and pepper to taste. Add heavy cream and cream cheese. Mix well; set aside.
2. In a large saucepan, cook pasta in boiling salted water until tender but firm. Remove from heat and drain. Sprinkle mixture over pasta. Mix well.

A&B Rigatoni with Garlic

1 pound rigatoni
5 tablespoons olive oil
2 cloves garlic, minced or pressed
Pinch of sea salt
Pinch of freshly ground pepper
3 sprigs rosemary

1. Cook pasta in boiling salted water until tender but firm.
2. While pasta is cooking, fry garlic, rosemary, salt, and pepper in oil until garlic is golden brown. Add 2 tablespoons of the water in which the rigatoni is cooking; stir. Remove rosemary from oil mixture.
3. When rigatoni is cooked, remove from heat and drain. Place in a warm bowl; mix with the flavored oil and serve immediately.

A&B Trenette with Pesto

1 pound trenette
4 garlic cloves, crushed
2 cups fresh basil leaves, crushed
Sea salt to taste
1 teaspoon olive oil
1 cup grated mozzarella cheese
1/2 cup pine nuts

1. Crush basil leaves with a mortar and pestle, gradually adding salt and garlic cloves. When all the garlic and basil is thoroughly crushed, start to add mozzarella cheese. Continue to grind until all the ingredients form a fairly thick consistency. Dilute with olive oil. Now the pesto sauce is ready.
2. Cook pasta in boiling salted water until tender but firm. Remove from heat and drain. Place trenette in a warm bowl and add pesto sauce; mix thoroughly until all noodles are evenly coated.

A
Rice

Bavarian A&B Rice
with Mushrooms

1-1/2 cups Basmati rice (or brown rice)
1 cup Portobello mushrooms, sliced
1 cup shitake mushrooms, sliced
1 cup chanterelle mushrooms, sliced
1 large onion, chopped
3 scallions, cut to 1-1/2-inch pieces, and pieces cut into stripes
1/2 cup parsley, finely chopped
3 tablespoons olive oil
2 tablespoons Teriyaki sauce
1/2 cup heavy sour cream
1/2 cup feta cheese, grated
Filtered water

1. Wash rice (especially brown rice) in a fine sieve until water is clear. In a large bowl, put rice and cover with water. Soak it for 10 minutes. Remove water, add hot water and cover rice with water 1/2-inch over rice. Cook on medium to low heat for 20 minutes until rice absorbed the water.

2. In a fry pan, heat oil; add onions, let cook until golden brown. Add Teriyaki sauce, stir it for 30 seconds. Add all mushrooms; simmer for 5 minutes, add heavy cream. Stir it frequently.
3. Add scallions and simmer it for further 5 minutes. Season with sea salt and pepper.
4. In a large bowl, place the rice. Create a small hole in the middle of the rice, pour mushrooms and sauce, sprinkle evenly with parsley and feta cheese. Serve warm.

A&B Rice with White Sauce

The following is the basic recipe for preparing rice. The A&B White Sauce on the following page can be used with almost any rice dish.

A&B Rice

Basic Recipe

1 cup natural (brown) rice (2 servings)
1-1/2 tablespoons butter
4 tablespoons olive oil
4 cups chicken broth (or 4 bouillon cubes, dissolved in 4 cups water)

In a medium saucepan, melt butter over medium-low heat. Add rice and cook, stirring, 2–3 minutes. Add 2 cups of broth (or bouillon). Cook rice, stirring, 5–6 minutes. Add 1 more cup broth. Cook until fluid is almost absorbed, 4–5 minutes. Gradually, add remaining broth. Cook, continuously stirring, until rice is tender but firm, about 10–15 minutes. Remove from heat. Let cool. OPTIONAL: Bring 2-1/2 cups water to boil. Add some sea salt and about 1 teaspoon olive oil or butter, if desired. Add 1 cup rice; stir until thoroughly blended with water. Reduce heat. Cover. Simmer about 20 minutes. Turn off heat. Fluff rice with fork.

A&B White Sauce
Basic Recipe

6 tablespoons butter
4 tablespoons whole wheat flour
1 cup heavy cream (diluted with 2 cups water)
Pinch of sea salt and freshly ground pepper
Pinch of grated nutmeg, optional

In a saucepan, melt butter over low heat. Slowly pour in flour as butter melts; stir until smooth. Pour in cream, stirring constantly for 15 minutes or until smooth and velvety. Increase heat and stir until sauce comes to a boil. Low simmer for 10 minutes more, stirring occasionally. Add salt, pepper, and nutmeg to taste. Whisk again until the sauce is smooth.

A&B Crispy
Rice Balls St. Tropez

1 cup brown rice
1-1/2 tablespoons butter
1/4 cup olive oil
4 cups chicken broth (or 4 bouillon cubes, dissolved in 4 cups water)
Wheat or soy flour
Bread crumbs
3 egg yolks
1/4 pound mozzarella cheese, cut into 20 cubes
1/4 cup feta cheese
1 tablespoon parsley, minced
1/8 tablespoon freshly ground pepper
1/4 teaspoon grated nutmeg

1. Prepare rice (basic recipe).
2. In a large bowl, beat 1 egg yolk. Add rice along with cheese, parsley, pepper, nutmeg. Blend well. Cover mixture and refrigerate at least 1 hour, until chilled.
3. In a small bowl, beat 2 egg yolks with 2 teaspoons water; set aside.

4. Scoop mixture. Place mozzarella in center. Shape rice with the palms of your hands into balls (1-1/2 inches) on a baking sheet. Roll balls in flour. Roll balls in egg yolks. Coat balls with bread crumbs. Place rice balls around the mozzarella. Cover with plastic wrap. Refrigerate for 2 hours.
5. In a heavy saucepan heat 3 inches of oil to 375°F. Place chilled rice balls in hot oil. Fry, occasionally turning, for 3–5 minutes, until golden brown. Remove with a spoon. Drain on paper towels. Serve at once.

A&B Rice Piazza San Marco

Rice (basic recipe)
A&B White Sauce (basic recipe)
1 cup raisins, soaked in water for 5 hours
1/2 cup almonds, chopped
Walnuts

1. Prepare rice; set aside.
2. Prepare A&B White Sauce. Mix rice with white sauce. Add raisins and almonds. Mix well. Garnish with walnuts.

Mediterranean A&B Rice with Broccoli

Rice (basic recipe)
1 bunch fresh broccoli, stems cut off
1/2 cup chopped olives, black and green
1/2 pound Canadian bacon, chopped
3 cloves garlic, minced or pressed
1/4 cup dry white wine
7-oz can chicken broth (or bouillon cubes)
1 cup A&B White Sauce
2 tablespoons butter
1/2 cup olive oil
1/2 cup fresh parsley, chopped
1 tablespoon basil

1. Prepare rice. Remove from heat. Place in a warm bowl.
2. Prepare A&B White Sauce.
3. In a saucepan, lightly brown oil, garlic, and bacon for 10 minutes. Add wine and let simmer over medium heat for 5 minutes. Add chicken broth and A&B White Sauce; simmer for 5 minutes. Add olives, basil, parsley, and butter; simmer another 3 minutes. Mix with rice. Mix well.

A&B Gilbert's Rice Salad

1 cup natural (brown) rice
4 cups lettuce (or any other greens), chopped
1 tomato, quartered
1 medium onion, quartered
1/2 cup green olives, sliced
1/2 cup walnuts, chopped
1 tablespoon olive oil
Vinegar to taste
1 teaspoon dried basil
1 teaspoon dried oregano
Sea salt to taste
Cayenne pepper to taste
Pepper to taste

1. Prepare rice (basic recipe). Let stand until rice is cool enough to be refrigerated. Refrigerate 1 hour.
2. Add lettuce, onion, tomato, olives, oil, vinegar, walnuts, basil, oregano. Season to taste. Mix well.

A
Couscous

A&B Couscous Tunisian

2 cups couscous
3 medium potatoes, cut in quarters
2 pounds pumpkin pulp or squash, cut in cubes
5 carrots, cut in halves
2 celery stalks, cut 3 to 4-inches long
1 green pepper
1 red pepper
2 cloves garlic
1 large onion,
1 bunch coriander, sliced
Dried coriander
Cumin
Saffron
Sea salt
Pepper
3 vegetable, beef, or chicken bouillon cubes
  (diluted with 3 cups of water)
Butter
Oil

1. In a large frying pan, cook onions in oil, stirring occasionally, until tender. Add pumpkin or squash. Add garlic, coriander, vegetables, salt, pepper, dried coriander, cumin, and saffron. Let cook; stir occasionally. Add 3 cups bouillon. Let cook, until tender. Set aside.

2. In a vegetable steamer, place couscous over boiling water, 30 minutes. Cook until tender. Remove from heat, but keep warm.
3. In a big bowl, place couscous. Pour vegetables and sauce over couscous. Serve warm.

Pizza

The following pages will supply the two basic recipes needed for creating the perfect A&B Pizza: the A&B Pizza Dough made from either whole wheat flour or frozen wheat bread dough and the A&B Pizza Sauce which replaces the common but chemically incompatible tomato sauce.

A&B Pizza Dough
Basic Recipe

2 cups whole wheat flour
1 tablespoon yeast
1-1/2 cups water
2 tablespoons olive oil
1 tablespoon butter
1 teaspoon sea salt

1. In a medium mixing bowl combine flour, yeast, oil, salt, and water. Stir mixture together with your hands until dough is firm but moist. If necessary, add more water 1 tablespoon at time. Let dough rest for 1 hour.
2. Knead dough again with your hands. Cover and let rise in a warm place for 20 minutes.
3. Preheat oven to 350°F. Sprinkle whole wheat flour over greased baking sheet.
4. Using a rolling pin, roll out dough on baking sheet. Arrange toppings.

A&B Pizza Sauce
Basic Recipe

1 cup ricotta cheese
3 cloves garlic
1/2 cup heavy cream
1 teaspoon oregano
1 teaspoon dried parsley
1 teaspoon basil
1 tablespoon olive oil

In a food processor, combine cheese, garlic, cream, oregano, parsley, and basil. Process until a paste forms. Slowly add oil; set aside until A&B Pizza Dough is ready.

A&B Pizza Romana

A&B Pizza Dough and A&B Pizza Sauce (basic recipe)
1 large onion, sliced
1 large green pepper, sliced
1/2 pound mushrooms, sliced
2 cloves garlic, grated
1/2 pound leeks, chopped
1/2 pound ewe's milk cheese
1 cup sour cream
1 tablespoon fresh basil, chopped (or 1 teaspoon dried)
Dried oregano to taste
1/2 pound olives
3 cups mozzarella, shredded

1. Prepare pizza dough
2. Prepare pizza sauce.
3. In a small saucepan, steam onions until tender but not brown. Add chopped leeks, 1 cup ewe's milk cheese, basil, and sour cream.
4. Spread mixture evenly over dough. Cut remaining ewe's milk cheese in quarters. Top pizza with olives, pepper, onions, mushrooms, and ewe's milk cheese. Sprinkle mozzarella and oregano evenly over the pizza. Bake at 350°F on lowest shelf (or the floor of a gas oven) until crust is firm and nicely brown at edges, 20–25 minutes. Cut into serving pieces and serve warm.

A&B Mozzarella Pizza

A&B Pizza Dough and A&B Pizza Sauce (basic recipe)
3 cups mozzarella cheese (about 12 ounces), shredded
2 tablespoons pine nuts

1. Prepare Pizza Dough.
2. Prepare Pizza Sauce.
3. Spread Pizza Sauce evenly over dough. Top with mozzarella and pine nuts. Place baking sheet on lowest shelf in oven (or the floor of a gas oven). Bake at 350°F until crust is firm and nicely brown, 15 to 20 minutes. Serve warm.

A&B Pizza Via Veneto

A&B Pizza Dough and A&B Pizza Sauce (basic recipe)
1 jar/can artichoke hearts
2 medium onions, sliced
1/4 cup vegetable or olive oil
3 cups mozzarella, shredded
1 tablespoon oregano, chopped fresh (or 1 teaspoon dried)
2 tablespoons olive oil

1. Prepare Pizza Dough.
2. Prepare Pizza Sauce.
3. In a large frying pan, cook onions in oil, stirring occasionally, until tender. Add artichokes, cheese, and oregano; set aside.
4. Spread Pizza Sauce evenly over dough. Top with artichoke hearts, mozzarella, and oregano. Drizzle remaining oil over pizza and bake at 350°F on lowest shelf (or the floor of a gas oven) until crust is firm and nicely brown at edges, 15–20 minutes. Serve warm.

A&B Pizza Napoli

A&B Pizza Dough and A&B Pizza Sauce (basic recipe)
1-1/2 cups feta cheese, shredded
Olives (any kind, quantity to taste)
3 cups mozzarella, shredded

1. Prepare Pizza Dough.
2. Prepare Pizza Sauce.
3. Spread Pizza Sauce evenly over dough. Top with feta and olives. Sprinkle mozzarella evenly over the pizza. Place baking sheet on lowest shelf in oven and bake until crust is firm and nicely brown, 15–20 minutes. Serve warm.

A&B Pizza Venetian

A&B Pizza Dough and A&B Pizza Sauce (basic recipe)
1 large eggplant
2 cups mozzarella, shredded
4 cloves garlic, chopped or crushed
1 large onion, chopped (for eggplants)
1 large onion, sliced into rings (for pizza)
1 green pepper, sliced
1 teaspoon oregano
1 teaspoon basil
1 teaspoon parsley
1/2 cup olive oil

1. Cut eggplant into 3/4-inch quarters. Put eggplant in a strainer. Sprinkle sufficient salt over eggplant. Let stand until fluid is removed, 45 minutes. In a large saucepan, cook eggplant in hot oil until brown. Add onions and garlic, turning, until eggplant is nicely brown; set aside.
2. Prepare Pizza Dough.
3. Prepare Pizza Sauce.
4. Spread Pizza Sauce over dough. Top with pieces of eggplant. Sprinkle oregano, parsley, and basil. Top with mozzarella and onion rings. Place baking sheet on lowest shelf in oven (or the floor of a gas oven) and bake at 350°F until crust is firm and nicely brown, 15–20 minutes. Serve warm.

A&B Pizza Milanese

A&B Pizza Dough and A&B Pizza Sauce (basic recipe)
1/2 pound mushrooms, sliced
2 large leeks, sliced
1 large onion, sliced into rings
1–2 pepper, sliced into rings
Olives (any kind, quantity to taste)
Sea salt

1. Prepare Pizza Dough and Pizza Sauce.
2. Spread sauce evenly over dough. Top with mushrooms, leeks, onion rings, pepper rings, and olives. Place baking sheet on lowest shelf in oven (or the floor of a gas oven) and bake at 350°F until crust is firm and nicely brown, 15–20 minutes. Serve warm.

Pizza A&B Four Seasons

A&B Pizza Dough and A&B Pizza Sauce (basic recipe)
Broccoli, quantity to taste
Cauliflower, quantity to taste
Mushrooms, quantity to taste
1/2 eggplant
1 large onion, sliced into rings
Olives (quantity to taste)
3 cups mozzarella, shredded

1. Cut eggplant into 3/4-inch quarters. Put eggplant in a strainer. Sprinkle sufficient salt over eggplant. Let stand until fluid is removed, 45 minutes. In a large saucepan, cook eggplant in hot oil until brown. Add onions and garlic, turning, until eggplant is nicely brown; set aside.
2. Prepare Pizza Dough.
3. Prepare Pizza Sauce.
4. Spread Pizza Sauce evenly over dough. Top with broccoli, cauliflower, mushrooms, eggplants, onions, olives. Sprinkle mozzarella evenly over the pizza. Place baking sheet on lowest shelf in oven (or the floor of a gas oven) and bake at 350°F until crust is firm and nicely brown, 15–20 minutes. Serve warm.

A

Potatoes

The potato is full of vitamin C, calcium, and phosphorus. However, the richest concentration of these healthy minerals is directly under the skin. To reap the potato's full health benefits cook them in their skins.

A&B Austrian Baked Potatoes "Arnold"

Potatoes, quantity to taste
Butter (1 tablespoon for each potato)
Sour cream, OR ready-to-buy fresh creamy Italian garlic dip OR fresh sour cream dip without preservatives
Aluminum wrap
Parsley and chives
Sea salt
Pepper

1. With a sharp knife, make a 1-inch cut across each potato. Season potatoes with salt and pepper to taste. Top each potato with a tablespoon of butter. Wrap each potato in aluminum wrap.
2. Preheat oven to 400°F. Place potatoes on baking sheet. Bake until tender, approximately 30 minutes.
3. In a bowl, combine sour cream with parsley and chives to taste. Serve warm (in its aluminum wrap).

A&B Potato Casserole

4 large potatoes, steamed and 1/4-inch sliced
4 zucchinis, 1/4-inch sliced
1 large onion, sliced
4 egg yolks
1/2 cup mozzarella, shredded
Herbs to taste
Dried parsley to taste
4 tablespoons butter or oil

1. In a vegetable steamer, place potatoes over boiling water, 20 minutes. Add zucchini. Cook until tender. Place potatoes in a large bowl. Let stand until potatoes are cool enough to handle. Peel and slice potatoes.
2. In a small bowl, whisk egg yolks. Add mozzarella. Mix well; set aside.
3. In a medium saucepan, cook onions in butter (or olive oil) until golden brown. Add potatoes and zucchini. Sprinkle egg mixture over potatoes and vegetables. Cook for another 3 minutes. Reduce heat. Cover saucepan. Let stand 15 minutes. Sprinkle herbs over casserole.

A&B Potato Salad Bavaria

4 large or 6 small potatoes, (any type)
1 onion, sliced
1/2 bunch parsley, chopped
Vinegar to taste
Olive oil to taste
Sea salt to taste
Pepper to taste

1. In a vegetable steamer, place potatoes over boiling water, 20 minutes. Cook until almost tender. Remove from heat. Place potatoes in a large bowl. Let stand until potatoes are cool enough to handle. Peel potatoes.
2. Cut potatoes into 1/2-inch quarters. Add oil, vinegar, salt, and pepper to taste. Mix well.

A&B Potato Salad d' Alsace

6 new potatoes, unpeeled
Beef salami, dice into cubes,), quantity to taste
(OPTIONAL: smoked fish)
1 fresh cucumber, sliced
1 large tomato, sliced in cubes
2 large pickles (sour or sweet dill), chopped into very thin slices
1/2 bunch chives, chopped
Scallions to taste, chopped
1 onion, chopped
Mayonnaise and/or chunky Blue Cheese dressing to taste
Olive or any other natural oil to taste
Vinegar to taste
Sea salt, pepper and celery salt to taste

1. In a vegetable steamer, place potatoes over boiling water for 20–30 minutes. Cook until tender. Remove from heat. Place potatoes in a large bowl. Let stand until potatoes are cool enough to handle. Peel potatoes. Cut potatoes into 1/2-inch cubes.
2. Add oil, vinegar, vegetables, pickled cucumbers, salami (or fish), and mayonnaise to potatoes. Mix well.

A&B Potato Salad Vienna

4 large or 6 small potatoes, unpeeled
1 can peas
4 carrots, chopped
1/2 bundle parsley, chopped
Mayonnaise to taste
Oil to taste
Vinegar to taste
Sea salt to taste
Pepper to taste
Garlic powder to taste

1. In a vegetable steamer, place potatoes over boiling water for 20–30 minutes. Cook until tender. Remove from heat.
2. Place potatoes in a large bowl. Let stand until potatoes are cool enough to handle. Peel potatoes. Cut potatoes into 1/2-inch cubes.
3. Add oil, vinegar, carrots, parsley, peas (drained), mayonnaise, salt, pepper, and garlic powder to potatoes. Mix well.

A&B Hungarian Potato Salad with Creamy Dressing

6 new potatoes, unpeeled
2 tablespoons butter
1 cup red cabbage, shredded
1–2 tablespoons mayonnaise
1/4 cup olive oil
1 large garlic clove, crushed through a press
1/2 tablespoon sea salt
1/4 teaspoon Hungarian or other paprika
1 tablespoon vinegar
1/2 teaspoon dried thyme
Fresh ground black pepper to taste

1. In a vegetable steamer, place potatoes over boiling water for 20 minutes. Cook until tender. Remove from heat. Place potatoes in a large bowl. Let stand until potatoes are cool enough to handle. Peel potatoes. Cut potatoes into 1/2-inch cubes.

2. In a small saucepan, melt butter. Pour butter over potatoes; add sea salt and paprika and mix well. Add cabbage; set aside.
3. Combine oil, vinegar, salt, garlic, celery salt, herbs, and mayonnaise. Blend well until dressing forms a paste. Pour dressing over potato salad.

A&B Austrian Potato Pancake

2 medium baking potatoes
1/2 small onion, chopped
1 tablespoon whole wheat flour
1/4 teaspoon baking powder
1/2 cup olive oil
1/2 cup sour cream
2 egg yolks
1 tablespoon minced fresh marjoram (or 1 teaspoon dried)
1/4 teaspoon sea salt
1/8 teaspoon freshly ground pepper

1. In a food processor, grate potatoes, flour, baking powder, and onion. Mix well.
2. Combine marjoram, egg yolks, salt, and pepper. Beat until well blended.
3. In a large frying pan, cook 2 tablespoons oil over medium heat. Drop small portions of potato mix into hot oil and flatten with back of a spoon. Cook, turning once, until golden brown on both sides, about 5 minutes. Drain on paper towels. Top each pancake with sour cream.

A&B New Potatoes Marseilles

5 new potatoes, unpeeled
2–3 tablespoons butter, melted
1/4 cup fresh parsley, chopped
Sea salt
Pepper

1. In a vegetable steamer, place potatoes over boiling water for 20 minutes. Cook until tender.
2. Remove from heat. Place potatoes in a large bowl. Let stand until potatoes are cool enough to handle. Peel potatoes.
3. Cut potatoes into 1/4-inch slices. Place on baking sheet and brush evenly with butter. Sprinkle with seasoning and place as close as possible to heat of broiler until crusty and golden, for 10 minutes. Sprinkle parsley over potatoes.

A&B Potato Salzburg with Sour Cream

10 small new potatoes, unpeeled
2–4 cups olive oil
1/2 cup sour cream
1/2 bunch chives, minced

1. Preheat oven to 400°F. Arrange potatoes on a baking sheet. Bake potatoes until tender, about 40 minutes. Place potatoes in a large bowl. Let stand until potatoes are cool enough to handle.
2. Peel potatoes. Halve potatoes. Cut a thin slice from the rounded bottom of each potato half so it will stand upright. Using a small spoon, scoop out center from each potato half, leaving a shell about 1/4 inch thick. Using a small spoon, fill each potato cavity with 2 teaspoons sour cream. Cook until heated through, about 10 minutes.

A&B Sweet Potato Bites

1 pound sweet potatoes (approximately 2-inch diameter)
2 tablespoons olive oil
1/3 cup sour cream

1. Preheat oven to 400°F.
2. Scrub potatoes and trim ends. Cut into 1/4-inch rounds.
3. Brush a baking dish with oil. Arrange sweet potato slices in a single layer; brush tops with remaining oil. Bake 15 minutes or until slices are golden brown on the bottom. Turn slices over. Cook until both sides are nicely brown, 10 minutes.
4. Top with sour cream.

A
Desserts

Banana Cream

2 pounds bananas
2 cups heavy cream, whipped
1/2 teaspoon vanilla
1/4 cup almonds, minced
Honey to taste
Raisins to taste

In a processor, combine bananas with whipped cream and 1/2 teaspoon vanilla. Process until mixture is firm. Garnish with raisins; sprinkle almonds over banana cream; refrigerate.

Fried Bananas

Bananas, cut in halves
Butter to taste
Almonds, chopped
2 tablespoons honey

In a frying pan, cook butter until golden brown. Add bananas. Fry until golden brown. Remove pan from heat. Sprinkle nuts, almonds, and honey over banana. Serve immediately.

A&B Banana Flambé

1 banana, sliced
2 tablespoons honey
2 tablespoons butter
Cognac to taste
Walnuts, chopped
Almonds, chopped

In a frying pan, place banana. Top with nuts and almonds. Fry until golden brown. Add butter. Let cook until melted. Add cognac. Burn alcohol. Serve flambé with nuts.

A&B Dessert
"Amadeus Mozart"

1 cup cottage cheese (or ricotta cheese)
1/2 cup soaked raisins for 5 hours
1/2 cup heavy cream, whipped
2 egg yolks (*)
1/8 cup hazelnuts

In a medium bowl, combine ingredients. Mix well.
Refrigerate.

*)There is some danger of salmonella from uncooked egg yolk.

A

Ice Cream

A&B Banana Ice Cream

2 cups heavy cream, whipped
1 pound bananas
2 tablespoons honey
1/2 cup walnuts, crushed

1. In a processor, combine whipped cream with fruit. Sweeten to taste.
2. In a plastic bowl, put mixture into freezer and chill at least 1 to 1-1/2 hours. Serve with whipped cream and decorate with walnuts.

A&B Vanilla Ice Cream

2 cups heavy cream, whipped
4 egg yolks (*)
2 tablespoons honey
1 teaspoon vanilla
Walnuts

1. In a processor combine whipped cream with egg yolks, honey, and vanilla. Process until mixture is foaming.
2. In a plastic bowl, put mixture into freezer and chill for at least 1 to 1-1/2 hours. Serve with whipped cream and decorate with walnuts.

(*)There is some danger of salmonella from uncooked egg yolks.

A&B Nut Ice Cream

2 cups heavy cream, whipped
4 egg yolks (*)
2 tablespoons honey
2 cups hazelnuts, crushed

1. In a processor combine whipped cream with egg yolks, honey, and hazelnuts. Process, until mixture is foaming.
2. In a plastic bowl, put mixture into freezer and chill at least for 1 to 1-1/2 hours. Serve with whipped cream and decorate with hazelnuts.

(*)There is some danger of salmonella from uncooked egg yolks.

A
Cakes
& Cookies

Moira's A&B Cheese Cake

1/2 cup whole wheat flour
1/2 cup unbleached flour
4 tablespoons butter
1/2 cup plus 1 tablespoon cream
1 tablespoon honey

CAKE FILLING
1 cup heavy cream
1 cup (filtered) water
4 tablespoons honey
2 egg yolks
1 pound Cottage cheese
1 package vanilla pudding powder
1 cup raisins

1. Preheat oven to 350°F.
2. Sift flour into a large bowl. Cut the butter into the flour by using a pastry cutter or two knifes until it is the consistency of course corn meal. Add the honey, egg yolk, cottage cheese and vanilla pudding powder. Mix all ingredients until they are blended. Do not over mix. Add the raisins.

3. On a floured clean surface, role out dough until it is large enough to cover a pie pan. Use your rolling pin to lift the dough. Roll the dough around the rolling pin and place over the pie pan. Fit it in the pie pan and remove excess dough (save for another use).
4. Mix all the cake ingredients until blended. Place ingredients on the crust.
5. Bake 30 minutes till it is golden on top. Let cool. Place in refrigerator until it thickens. Serve and enjoy.

A&B Blueberry Cookies

Same dough as cheese cake
1 pound blueberries

1. Preheat oven to 300°F.
2. Knead dough. Place dough on baking tin. Cut into squares. Fill each dough square with blueberries; fold over into cookies.
3. On a baking sheet, arrange cookies. Bake for 10 minutes.

A&B Raisin Cookies

Same dough as cheese cake
1/2 pound ricotta cheese
1 cup raisins, soaked in water for 5 hours

1. Preheat oven to 300°F.
2. Combine ricotta cheese with raisins. Mix well.
3. Knead dough. Place dough on baking tin. Cut into squares and fill with mixture.
4. On a baking sheet, arrange cookies. Bake for 10 minutes.

A&B Nut Cookies

1/4 pound rolled oats
1/4 pound butter
4 tablespoons honey
1 egg yolk
1/2 teaspoon baking powder
1/2 pound crushed hazelnuts

1. Preheat oven to 300°F.
2. Combine ingredients. Mix dough well.
3. On a baking sheet, place little portions of dough, about 1 teaspoon each. Garnish cookies with hazelnuts.
4. Bake cookies for 10 minutes, not too dark.

A&B Banana Cake

1 cup whole wheat flour
1 teaspoon yeast
2 bananas, mashed
1/4 pound butter
3 tablespoons honey
2 egg yolks
1/4 pound walnuts, chopped

1. Preheat oven to 300°F.
2. Whisk butter, honey, egg yolks until foaming. Add whole wheat flour, yeast, and mashed bananas.
3. Place mixture in a bread pan or baking pan. Sprinkle with chopped walnuts.
4. Bake cake for 20–25 minutes. Reduce heat. Let stand 2 minutes. Remove from heat; cut in pieces. Let cool.

A&B Honey Pancakes

1/4 cup oil
2 egg yolks
2 cups whole wheat flour
1/2 teaspoon baking soda
1 pinch salt
1-1/2–2 cups water
1/2 pound ricotta or cottage cheese
1/2 cup raisins
1 tablespoon honey

1. Beat the egg yolks and oil together.
2. Combine flour, soda, and salt. Add to eggs.
3. Add water until batter is of desired consistency. Make pancakes on a hot griddle or frying pan coated with a little oil.
4. For topping, combine cheese, honey and raisins. Serve over pancakes.

"B"

B

Soups

A&B Chicken Soup

5 pounds stewing chicken, cut up
6 cups (filtered) water
3 stalks celery, cut up
1 small onion, cut up
1/4 teaspoon salt
1/8 teaspoon pepper
1 bay leaf
16 ounces Italian peeled tomatoes (can), cut up
3 medium carrots, cut into julienne strips
1/2 cup onions, chopped
4 teaspoons instant chicken bouillon granules (sold in a jar)
1 cup zucchini, halved lengthwise and sliced

1. In a saucepan, combine chicken pieces, water, onion, celery, salt, pepper, and bay leaf. Bring to a boil. Reduce heat and simmer, covered, for 2 hours until chicken is tender. Remove chicken from broth. Let stand until chicken is cool enough to handle; then cut off meat and cube chicken; set aside.
2. Meanwhile, strain broth, discarding vegetables and bay leaf. Return broth to oven. Stir in tomatoes, onion, carrots, and bouillon. Simmer, covered, for 20 minutes until carrots are almost tender.
3. Add chicken to broth mixture along with zucchini. Simmer, covered, about 5 minutes until vegetables are tender.

B
Hors
d'oeuvre

Avocados with Shrimp

1 large avocado (1/2 for every person)
1 can shrimp, drained
4 tablespoons lemon juice
1 bunch dill, chopped
4 tablespoons olive oil
Salt to taste
Pepper to taste

1. Using a sharp knife, cut avocado in half. Remove pit.
2. In a medium bowl, combine lemon juice, oil, salt, and pepper to taste. Mix well.
3. Arrange shrimp on avocado. Top with dill. Pour mixture over avocado and dill. Serve immediately or cover with plastic wrap to prevent avocado from darkening. Refrigerate.

B
Salads

A&B Waldorf Astoria Salad

2 cups diced apples (2 medium apples)
2 sweet oranges, diced (without seeds)
1/2 pound cooked chicken, diced
3/4 cup celery, coarsely chopped
1 cup mayonnaise
1 cup sour cream
4 tablespoons heavy cream, whipped
1/2 cup coarsely chopped walnuts
1 dash cognac
2 tablespoons lemon juice (or vinegar)
1 dash salt

In medium bowl, combine all ingredients (except whipped cream, sour cream, and walnuts). Mix well. Chill thoroughly. Add whipped cream, sour cream, and walnuts before serving. Serve on lettuce. Refrigerate leftovers.

A&B Hawaiian Chicken Salad

1/2 pound cooked chicken (or leftovers), diced
2 cups pineapple, diced
1 cup mayonnaise
Dash vinegar
Dash pepper
Pinch garlic salt
Pinch nutmeg

In medium bowl, combine all ingredients; mix well. Chill thoroughly. Serve on lettuce; top with diced pineapple.

A&B Peking Chicken Salad

1 pound cooked (or fried) chicken (or any kind of poultry), diced
2 oranges, diced (without seeds)
1 peel of orange, grated
2 cups mayonnaise
1 cup almonds, cut in halves
Dash cognac
Pinch nutmeg

In a large bowl, combine all ingredients; mix well. Chill thoroughly. Serve on lettuce; garnish with orange slices.

A&B Carrot Salad d' Alsace

1 pound large carrots
1/4 pound cooked ham, quartered
2 oranges, juice
1 peel of orange, grated
2 cups mayonnaise
Dash garlic salt
Dash pepper
Dash nutmeg

Cut carrots into 1/8-inch slices. Combine ham, with juice of grated oranges and grated peel of oranges; add mayonnaise. Mix well. Add to carrots. Chill thoroughly. Serve on lettuce.

Swiss A&B Cheese Salad

1/2 pound Swiss cheese, thinly sliced
2 medium onions, thinly sliced into rings
Olive oil to taste
Vinegar to taste
Salt to taste
Pepper to taste

In medium bowl, combine all ingredients. Add salt and pepper to taste. Mix well.

Sylvia's A&B Tuna Salad

1 (6-1/2 ounce) can tuna (in oil or water)
1/4 cup capers, cut in halves
3 tablespoons onion, chopped
2 tablespoons mustard
1/2 cup pickled cucumbers, diced
1/3 cup parsley, chopped
Olive oil, quantity to taste
1 teaspoon fresh lemon juice (or vinegar)
1/4 teaspoon pepper
Salt to taste
Garlic salt to taste

In a medium bowl, mash tuna with oil and mustard. Add onions, lemon juice, pickled cucumber dices, capers, salt and pepper. Mix well. Serve on lettuce. Garnish with remaining capers,or pickled cucumber slices.

Bavarian Sausage Salad

1/2 pound Bologna sausage, sliced
2 medium onions, thinly sliced into rings
Olive oil to taste
Vinegar to taste
Salt to taste
Pepper to taste

Cut across sausage in 1/4-inch slices. Mix with onion slices. Add oil, vinegar, salt and pepper. Mix well.

A&B Chef Salad

Lettuce (quantity to taste)
Tomatoes, sliced or diced into cubes
Cucumber, thinly sliced
Broccoli, sliced
Cauliflower, sliced
Carrots, thinly sliced
Onions, sliced or diced into cubes
1–2 boiled eggs, sliced
Swiss cheese, thinly sliced
Smoked ham, sliced
Cooked turkey or chicken, rectangular sliced
Oil to taste
Vinegar to taste
Salt to taste
Pepper to taste
Mayonnaise (OPTIONAL: dip or dressing)

Cut up vegetables. In a large bowl, combine all vegetables, smoked ham, and turkey or chicken. Add oil, vinegar, salt, and pepper. Add mayonnaise (or dip or dressing). Mix well.

B Menus

The following "B" dishes can be served with any variety of vegetable except potatoes and kale. Other ideal "B" salads include, honey melon and any other B-fruit; avocados with shrimp, vinegar, oil, and dill; shrimp cocktail with mayonnaise; mixed A&B salad; tuna salad; Waldorf Astoria salad; chicken salad with pineapple and mayonnaise; cheese of any kind; fruit salad; apple dessert with whipped cream; and ice cream with whipped cream and other desserts.

To keep your BioChemical Machine healthy, eat strong base-building foods (fruits, salads, vegetables) with the acid-building cooked meats and fish.

Poultry should not be marinated with sugar, syrup, or sauces containing sugars. You may marinate with soy flour mixed with egg yolk.

A&B Aubergine à la Ciel, Soleil et la Mere

2 medium eggplants
1-1/2 pounds tomatoes, diced
2 medium onions, slice into rings
2 cloves garlic, crushed through a press
2 tablespoon olive oil
1 tablespoon parsley, chopped
1/4 cinnamon stick
1 bay leaf
Sea salt
Pepper
1/2 cup chopped almonds

1. Preheat the oven to 400°F.
2. Roast eggplants for about 10 minutes, turning frequently.
3. Pull off the skins, halve the eggplants lengthwise, carefully scoop out and reserve the flesh.

4. In a saucepan, heat oil, sauté onions and garlic. Add tomatoes. Season with salt and pepper to taste. Add cinnamon stick and bay leaf, cook for 5 minutes. Add coarsely diced eggplant flesh, cook for further 5 minutes. Remove bay leaf and cinnamon. Add parsley and almonds.
5. Stuff eggplant shells with this mixture.
6. On a greased baking pan, place eggplants.
7. Turn down the heat to 350°F of the preheated oven. Bake for about 20 minutes. Serve warm.

A&B L' Aubergine Bretagne

2 large (or 4 small) eggplants
6 cloves garlic, crushed through a press
2 medium tomatoes, pureed
4 small onions, chopped
1 cup olive oil
1 bunch parsley, chopped
1 bunch cilantro, chopped
Sea salt to taste
Pepper to taste
Celery salt to taste

1. With a sharp knife, remove stem end of eggplants. Cut eggplants in 1/2-inch slices.
2. Chop cilantro and parsley. Puree tomatoes. Add garlic. Mix well.
3. In a large saucepan, heat oil. Place eggplants. Fry until brown.
4. Preheat oven to 300°F.
5. On a baking sheet, place eggplants. Sprinkle tomato-cilantro-parsley mixture over eggplants. Bake for 20 minutes, until crispy. Season to taste. Serve warm.

B

Minced Meat

A&B Aubergine à la Cairo

2 large eggplants (long style), washed
2 middle-sized tomatoes, chopped
1 large onion, chopped
1/2 bunch cilantro, chopped
1 pound minced meat
1/2 cup pine nuts
2 glove of garlic, crushed through a press
2 teaspoons oregano
1 teaspoon cumin (powder)
1 teaspoon coriander (powder)
1/2 teaspoon cinnamon (powder)
3 tablespoon olive oil
Sea salt to taste
Pepper to taste

1. With a sharp knife, cut eggplants in two halves.
2. With a tablespoon, carve 1-inch into the middle of the eggplant so that you will have a small portion of eggplants, set aside.
3. Sprinkle eggplants with sea salt. Put eggplants in a sieve. Let stand for at least one hour to eliminate liquid.
4. Chop small portion of eggplants into small cubes, set aside.
5. In a small frying pan, heat 1 teaspoon olive oil, add pine nuts and roast it until golden brown.

6. In a large frying pan, heat olive oil, add onions. Let fry until golden brown.
7. Add minced meat, mix it well with onions. Let cook until well done.
8. Add cilantro and chopped small portion of eggplants and tomatoes. Mix well and let simmer for 20 minutes, stirring frequently.
9. Add all spices and pine nuts, mix well. Turn off the heat. Set mixture aside.
10. Preheat oven to 350°F.
11. Brush eggplants with olive oil. Spread garlic over eggplants.
12. In a baking pan, place eggplants evenly. Put baking pan into the oven. Let cook for 20 minutes.
13. Take baking pan out from the oven. Fill the carved parts of the eggplants with the mixture.
14. Return baking pan into oven. Let bake for another 20 minutes. Serve warm.

A&B Meatloaf

2-1/2 pounds minced beef
1 red bell paprika, chopped very small
2 celery sticks, chopped very small
2 middle-sized onions, chopped very small
1 cup cilantro, chopped
1 cup parsley, chopped
2 cloves garlic, crushed through a press
1 tablespoon Teriyaki sauce
1 cup Soy flour
3 egg yolks
2 teaspoons sea salt
1 teaspoon pepper
1 teaspoon marjoram
6 green olives without pits, cut in two halves
1 tablespoon olive oil
4 bay leaves

1. In a large bowl, put beef and add all ingredients from red bell paprika to marjoram. Mix it very well with your hand.
2. Preheat oven to 350°F.

3. In a loaf pan, grease pan with olive oil and place mixture evenly.
4. Decorate olives on top of the beef and put the bay leaves decoratively 1-inch deep into the mixture.
5. Put meat loaf in the preheated oven. Bake for at least 1 hour until crispy brown.
6. Remove meat loaf from the pan. Serve warm with French green beans and Classic Green Salad.

Minced Meat St. Tropez

1-1/2 pounds ground beef
1-1/2 pounds vegetables (carrots, celery, tomatoes, onions), sliced
1 whole egg
1 cup bouillon (or vegetable water or regular water)
1 tablespoon butter (or olive oil)
1/4 teaspoon cayenne pepper
1 pinch celery salt
1 pinch nutmeg

1. In a small frying pan, combine butter and onions until lightly brown. Add vegetables and bouillon (or vegetable water or water); cook until vegetables are tender.
2. In a small bowl, combine ground beef, egg, salt, and pepper. Mix well.
3. Roll ground beef (1/2-inch) on aluminum wrap. Place vegetables in center of meat. Fold over vegetables with meat.
4. Preheat oven to 350°F. Place meat on baking sheet. Bake meat until tender, approximately 30 minutes. Remove from heat, cut in slices, and serve with salad.

French A&B Cabbage Roll

1 large white cabbage
2 pounds ground beef
1/2 pound mushrooms (optional)
2 whole eggs
1/2 cup sour cream
3 large onions, chopped
1 clove garlic, crushed through a press
4 tablespoons butter or olive oil
1 pinch thyme
1 pinch cumin and fennel herbs
1 pinch pepper and 1 pinch sweet Hungarian or other paprika
1 pinch sea salt

1. Place cabbage in a vegetable steamer, for 5–7 minutes (or in boiling water). Cook until leaves are tender when pierced with tip of sharp knife. Separate tender leaves. Cut leaves in quarters.
2. In a small frying pan, cook onions until golden brown.

3. In a big bowl, combine beef, onions, eggs, and spices. Mix well.
4. On a big plate, arrange leaves and form mixture into balls. Arrange beef mixture on prepared cabbage leaves. Wrap cabbage around meat. Bind each with string.
5. In a large frying pan, melt 4 tablespoons of butter over medium heat. Add onions, and cabbage rolls. Cook cabbage rolls, turning, until brown. When golden brown, add sour cream and 1/2 cup of water. Let stand on slow fire, 45 minutes. Serve warm.

Farmer's A&B Meat Balls

1 pound ground beef
1 large onion, cut in halves
1 large onion, quartered
2 tablespoons soy flour
1 whole egg
2 cloves garlic, chopped
1 tablespoon butter
1/4 cup capers
3 bay leaves
1 pinch herb salt and 1 pinch pepper
1 cup vegetable broth

1. In a large bowl, combine ground beef with egg and spices, until blended. Mix well. Form meatballs. Set aside.
2. In medium saucepan, bring 1 cup vegetable broth to a boil. Add 1 onion (cut in halves), garlic, bay leaves and meatballs. Cook on medium heat, for 30 minutes until browned.
3. In a medium frying pan, for the sauce, melt 1 tablespoon butter over medium heat. Mix soy flour, 1 cup vegetable water, sour cream, and capers. Mix until well blended. Simmer until a thick sauce is formed. Serve with green peas and carrots.

French Stuffed A&B Peppers

2 pounds ground beef
2 middle-size onions, sliced
2 middle-size onions, cut in halves
8 green peppers (or 8 zucchini or 8 large tomatoes)
5 cloves garlic, crushed through the press
   (optional: 2 teaspoons garlic powder)
1/2 bunch parsley, chopped
1/2 bunch cilantro, chopped
1/2 bunch dill, chopped
1 large lemon, juice of
2 tablespoons butter (or olive oil)
1 cup sour cream
1 cup of water
1 bouillon cube (beef, chicken, or vegetable)
1 pinch celery salt
1 pinch cumin
1 pinch cayenne pepper
1 pinch saffron

1. In a food processor or blender combine parsley, cilantro, garlic, and dill. Process until a puree forms.
2. In a big bowl, combine meat, eggs, puree, and spices (except saffron and lemon). Blend well.
3. With a sharp knife, cut off green pepper tops. Carefully remove seeds and veins, leaving stems intact.
4. Stuff green pepper with mixture.
5. Preheat oven to 350°F.

6. On a large baking sheet, melt 2 tablespoons butter (or olive oil); bake 1 onion, cut in halves, until softened. Arrange vegetables.
7. In a small frying pan, cook 1 cup of water and add 1 bouillon cube, saffron, and lemon juice. Add to vegetables. Bake until vegetables absorb most of the juice. Remove from oven. Add sour cream. Let stand 20 minutes. Serve warm.

Mediterranean A&B Meatballs

2 pounds ground beef
2 onions, chopped
2 onions, sliced
2 celery stalks, minced (food processor)
3–4 cloves garlic
1/2 bunch parsley
1 large can Italian peeled tomatoes
Butter to taste
Soy sauce to taste
Sea salt to taste
Pepper to taste
Celery salt to taste
Oregano to taste
Basil to taste

1. In a food processor or blender combine chopped onions, celery stalks, garlic, parsley, salt, pepper, celery salt, oregano, and basil. Process vegetables. Add meat and spices. Process until a puree forms. Form meatballs.

2. In a frying pan, combine butter and sliced onions until lightly brown. Add salt, pepper, oregano, parsley, celery salt, basil. Mix well. Add Italian peeled tomatoes; chop while cooking. Add meatballs and cook (low), turning, about 1 hour. Add soy sauce to taste.
3. Serve warm with mixed vegetables, such as carrots, green beans and zucchini, and Classic Green Salad.

B

Meat

A&B Beef à la Napoli

3 pounds ground beef
1 large white cabbage, sliced
1 cup shredded mozzarella cheese
1 medium onion, chopped
1/2 cup olive oil
1 can (14 ounces) Italian peeled tomatoes
1 can (8 ounces) tomato sauce
1/2 cup soy flour
1 teaspoon sea salt
1 teaspoon celery salt
1 teaspoon sea salt
2 teaspoons caraway seeds
2 apples, peeled, cored and chopped

1. Mix soy flour, sea salt, and caraway seeds. Mix well.
2. Form balls from the beef; roll them in the Soy flour mixture.
3. In a large frying pan, heat oil over medium heat. Add meat balls and cook, turning, until brown.
4. Preheat oven to 350°F.

5. In the same frying pan, cook onions about 3 minutes, until tender. Add tomatoes, tomato sauce, apples and sea salt. Bring to a boil. Add cabbage and mix well. Spoon mixture over meat.
6. Cover with foil and bake 1 hour, until meat is tender.
7. Remove foil; sprinkle mozzarella cheese over meat. Return to oven for about 5 minutes, until cheese melts.

Zurich A&B "Geschnetzeltes"

1-1/2 pounds beef or veal
1 pound mushrooms, sliced
1 can green peas, drained
2 cups heavy cream
Butter to taste
2 large onions, chopped
4 cloves garlic, crushed through a press
Celery salt to taste
Garlic powder to taste
Sea salt to taste
Pepper to taste

1. Cut meat in 1/2-inch slices. Season with celery salt and pepper.
2. In a small frying pan, combine butter, onions and garlic until lightly brown. Add meat and cook, turning, until brown. Reduce heat and add mushrooms, spices and heavy cream. Cook, stirring occasionally, about 1 hour. Add peas and season to taste.

A&B Cotoletta Milanese

1/2 pound ground beef or veal cutlets
8 oz. cream cheese
Butter
1 pinch nutmeg
1 pinch onion powder
1 pinch sea salt
1 pinch pepper
1 pinch celery salt
1 lemon, juice

1. Season both sides of meat to taste.
2. In a frying pan, melt butter over medium heat. Add meat. Cook, turning, until golden brown, approximately 10 minutes. Top with lemon juice.
3. Cut cream cheese into 1/8-inch slices and arrange over meat. Serve with vegetables and salad.

King Arthur's A&B Roast with Red Cabbage

5–6 pound roast beef, sliced
2 large onions, sliced
5 cloves garlic, crushed through a press
4 bay leaves
2 cups sour (or heavy) cream
3 tablespoons olive oil
4 cups water
1 bouillon cube (vegetable, chicken, or beef)
Red wine to taste

1. In a frying pan, cook onions, oil, and garlic until brown.
2. Add meat and red wine. Cook for 2 minutes.
3. Add 4 cups of water and 1 bouillon cube. Cook meat, covered, occasionally stirring, until tender. Add sour (or heavy) cream.
4. Serve with red cabbage and salad.

Austrian A&B Meat Hotchpotch

2 **pounds beef, diced**
2 **large onions, sliced**
2 **large zucchinis, sliced**
4 **large carrots, sliced**
1 **eggplant, diced**
1 **clove garlic, minced**
2 **tomatoes, coarsely chopped**
1 **cup sour cream**
2 **bunch leeks, chopped**
1 **bunch cilantro, chopped**
3 **tablespoons butter**
1/4 **teaspoon sea salt**
1 **pinch pepper**
1 **pinch celery salt**
1 **pinch garlic powder**

1. In a large frying pan, melt 3 tablespoons butter over medium heat. Add onions and cook until golden brown, about 5 minutes.
2. Add meat, turning, until brown. Add vegetables and garlic. Cook, covered, over medium heat. Season with salt and pepper to taste. Add fresh sour cream. Serve warm.

B

Poultry

Classic A&B Roast Chicken

1 middle-sized whole chicken
1 medium onion, thickly sliced
1 small onion, diced
2 carrots, thickly sliced
2 zucchinis, sliced
2 tablespoons butter
2 tablespoons olive oil
1 tablespoon dried thyme
1 tablespoon Soy flour
1 cup bouillon
Sea salt to taste
Pepper to taste

1. Rinse and dry the chicken.
2. Preheat oven to 350°F. Season chicken with sea salt and pepper inside and out. Put onions and thyme inside cavity and tie legs together. Rub butter all over chicken.
3. In a large oval gratin dish or shallow roasting pan, put oil. Scatter sliced onion, zucchini, and carrot around the dish. Place chicken on top.

4. Roast chicken in oven until it is golden brown.
5. Remove to a serving platter and cover with foil to keep warm.
6. Remove all but 2 tablespoons fat from pan. Place over medium heat, add soy flour, bouillon, and cook, stirring until thickened. Season with sea salt and pepper to taste. Strain into a gravy boat and serve with chicken.

Traditional A&B Roast Chicken & Summer Vegetables

1 middle-sized whole chicken
4 carrots, peeled and cut into 1-inch pieces
1/4 white cabbage, sliced
1 red pepper, sliced
4 small onions, diced
2 tablespoons butter
1 pinch sea salt and pepper
1 cup (dry) white wine
1 teaspoon dried rosemary
1 teaspoon dried oregano

1. Preheat oven to 375°F.
2. Season chicken inside and out with salt and pepper. Place 1/2 teaspoon rosemary in cavity. Tie legs together and rub butter over skin. Place in a large roasting pan.
3. Roast chicken for 15 minutes. Arrange vegetables around chicken. Sprinkle remaining rosemary and oregano over chicken and vegetables.
4. Pour wine over all and bake 1 hour and 15 minutes with pan drippings. Add water as soon as wine evaporates. Serve warm.

Chicken "Aloha A&B"

1 middle-sized whole chicken
2 tablespoons butter
2 tablespoons olive oil
Pineapple, diced
1/2 teaspoon dried thyme
1/2 teaspoon dried oregano
Sea salt and pepper to taste
Dry white wine

1. Preheat oven to 350°F. Season chicken inside and out with salt and pepper. Place 1/2 teaspoon thyme in cavity. Tie legs together and rub butter over skin. Place in a large roasting pan.
2. Roast chicken for 15 minutes. Arrange diced pineapple around chicken. Sprinkle remaining thyme over chicken. Pour dry white wine over all and bake 1 hour and 15 minutes. Add water (or cream) as soon as wine evaporates.

A&B Roast Chicken Milanese

1 middle-sized whole chicken
1 garlic clove, split in half
1 lemon, sliced
1 lemon, squeezed for juice
1 small onion, diced
Sea salt and pepper to taste

1. Preheat oven to 350°F.
2. Rinse chicken inside and out; pat dry.
3. Season inside and out with sea salt and pepper. Rub garlic over the skin; then place inside cavity. Stuff sliced lemon and onion inside cavity. Tie legs together and pour lemon juice over the chicken. Place chicken, breast side up, in a roasting pan.
4. Bake 1 hour and 15 minutes, until juices run clear.

A&B Chicken Côte d' Azur

1 middle-sized whole chicken
1/4 pound mushrooms, sliced
3 tablespoons parsley, chopped
3 tablespoons cilantro, chopped
1 egg yolk, beaten
2 tablespoons parsley, chopped
2 teaspoons grated lemon peel
1 tablespoon fresh lemon juice
1 garlic clove, crushed through a press
Sea salt and pepper to taste
Filtered water

1. Preheat oven to 350°F.
2. In a large frying pan, melt 4 tablespoons of the butter over medium heat. Add onion and mushrooms and cook until onion is tender and mushrooms are lightly brown, about 5 minutes. Remove from heat. Add egg, parsley, cilantro, lemon peel, and 3/4 cup (filtered) water. Mix well.

3. In a small saucepan, melt remaining 3 tablespoons butter. Add garlic and lemon juice; set aside.
4. In a large frying pan, place chicken. Tie legs together. Season with sea salt and pepper. Brush with butter.
5. Roast for 1-1/2 hours, basting occasionally, until chicken is tender.

A&B Ricotta Chicken

1 middle-sized chicken
1 cup ricotta cheese
5 tablespoons butter
1 large onion, chopped
2 cups grated zucchini
1 garlic clove, crushed through a press
1 egg, beaten
1 teaspoon sea salt
1/2 teaspoon pepper
1 teaspoon dried basil
1/2 teaspoon dried oregano
1/2 teaspoon dried marjoram

1. Preheat oven to 350°F.
2. In a large frying pan, melt 3 tablespoons butter over medium heat. Add onion and cook until tender, about 3 minutes. Add zucchini and cook until wilted, about 3 minutes longer; remove from heat.
3. Mix ricotta cheese, marjoram, egg, salt, and pepper. Mix well.
4. Put stuffing in the chicken.
5. In a small saucepan, melt remaining 2 tablespoons butter. Add garlic, basil, and oregano. Brush chicken with butter. Roast 1-1/2 hours until tender and juices run clear, basting every 20 or 30 minutes.

A&B Parmesan Chicken Breast

1-1/2 pounds chicken breast
3 tablespoons butter
2 tablespoons soy flour
1 cup sweet cream (diluted with filtered water)
1/2 cup grated Parmesan cheese
1/2 cup Swiss cheese, shredded
Sea salt to taste
Pepper to taste

1. Preheat oven to 350°F.
2. Season chicken breast with salt and pepper. In a large frying pan, melt butter over medium heat. Add chicken breast and cook, turning, until brown, about 10 minutes.
3. Sprinkle 1/4 cup of the Parmesan cheese over bottom of a medium baking dish. Arrange chicken in dish.

4. In same frying pan, whisk soy flour into pan drippings. Cook, stirring, for 1 minute. Gradually add cream and cook, stirring constantly, until smooth and thick.
5. Remove from heat and stir in Swiss cheese. Pour sauce over chicken.
6. Top chicken with remaining 1/4 cup Parmesan cheese. Bake for 45 minutes, until chicken is tender.

A&B Chicken with Spinach

2 cups chopped cooked chicken
3 tablespoons butter
3 tablespoons soy flour
1-3/4 cups cream (diluted with filtered water)
1 pound spinach, chopped
1 cup grated Parmesan cheese
10 slices Swiss cheese
1/2 pound mushrooms, halved
1 teaspoon sea salt
1 teaspoon pepper
1/4 teaspoon nutmeg
2 tablespoons water
Paper towels

1. Preheat oven to 350°F.
2. Place spinach in a large saucepan with 2 tablespoons water. Cover and steam until tender, about 3 minutes. Drain well; press between paper towels to squeeze out excess water. Transfer to a medium baking dish.

3. In a large saucepan, melt butter over medium heat. Stir in flour and cook for 1 minute. Gradually whisk in cream and soy flour. Add salt, pepper, and nutmeg. Cook, stirring constantly, until mixture thickens and comes to a boil. Reduce heat to low, add Swiss cheese, and cook until melted.
4. Remove sauce from heat. Add chicken and mushrooms. Pour over spinach.
5. Sprinkle Parmesan cheese over chicken. Bake for 20 minutes, until bubbly and lightly brown on top.

A&B Chicken Thighs

8 pieces chicken thighs
1/4 cup Parmesan cheese, grated
1/4 cup Swiss cheese, grated
2 tablespoons butter
4 tablespoons butter, melted
1 cup grated carrots
1 cup broccoli, chopped
1 cup zucchini, chopped
1 onion, chopped
Sea salt to taste
Pepper to taste
Oregano to taste

1. Preheat oven to 350°F.
2. Place chicken on a baking sheet. Sprinkle the chicken with butter and Parmesan cheese. Bake until chicken is tender, for 45 minutes.
3. In a frying pan, melt butter over medium-high heat. Add carrots, broccoli, zucchini and onion and cook, tossing often, 5 minutes, until broccoli is crisp-tender.
4. Before serving, sprinkle Swiss cheese over the chicken, bake for another 5 minutes to allow melting.
5. Serve warm.

A&B Chicken Wings & Blue Cheese Dip

24 whole chicken wings
2–4 cups vegetable oil
4 tablespoons butter
2 tablespoons Soy flour
2–5 tablespoons hot pepper sauce
1 tablespoon vinegar
Celery sticks
1 tablespoon grounded cumin
Sea salt to taste
Pepper to taste
1 cup of blue cheese dip

1. Rinse chicken and pat dry. Cut off and discard pointed tip of each wing and halve wings at the main join.
2. Mix salt, pepper and cumin with Soy flour. Roll chicken wings in the mixture.
3. In a large, heavy saucepan, heat oil.

4. Cook the wings, in batches without crowding, until crisp and golden, about 10 minutes. Drain well on paper towels.
5. In a small saucepan, melt butter over medium heat. Stir in hot sauce and vinegar. Mound wings on a serving plate and pour hot butter sauce over them. Serve at once, with celery sticks and blue cheese dip.

A&B Chicken Monte Carlo

1 middle-sized whole chicken
2 tablespoons butter
2 tablespoons chopped onion
2 tablespoons chopped parsley
1/2 cup dry white wine
1/4 cup grated Parmesan cheese
1 teaspoon paprika
1/4 teaspoon dried marjoram
1/4 teaspoon dried tarragon
1/2 teaspoon dried chives
1/2 teaspoon dried oregano

1. Preheat oven to 350°F.
2. In a small saucepan, melt butter over medium heat. Add onion and cook until tender, about 3 minutes. Stir in parsley, oregano, chives, tarragon, marjoram, and wine. Boil 5 minutes, until sauce is reduced by one-third.
3. Arrange chicken in a medium baking dish. Brush herb sauce over chicken. Sprinkle with Parmesan cheese and paprika. Bake 45 minutes, until tender.

A&B Chicken Las Vegas

1 middle-sized whole chicken, cut up
2 large garlic bulbs, separated into cloves
3 celery stalks, cut into 1-inch lengths
4 slices pineapple, chopped into dices
1/4 cup olive oil
1/4 cup dry white wine
1 cup heavy cream
2 tablespoons parsley, chopped
2 tablespoons fresh basil, chopped, or 1/2 teaspoon dried
1/4 tablespoon freshly ground pepper
1/4 teaspoon sweet Hungarian pepper
3 tablespoons fresh lemon juice
1/2 teaspoon grated lemon rind
Sea salt to taste

1. Preheat oven to 375°F.
2. In a medium baking pan, arrange chicken skin side up. Sprinkle garlic cloves and celery over chicken.
3. Mix wine, oil, salt, pepper, basil, lemon juice, and sweet Hungarian pepper. Add pineapples and heavy cream. Mix well. Pour over chicken. Sprinkle lemon rind on top.
4. Bake, covered, for 40 minutes.
5. Uncover and bake for further 15 minutes, until chicken is tender. Serve warm.

A&B Chicken Santa Fe

3 pounds chicken, cut up
6 tablespoons butter
1/2 cup grated white Cheddar cheese
1 can (28 ounces) Italian peeled tomatoes, drained and finely chopped
1-1/4 cups soy flour
2 cups cream
2 tablespoons olive oil
3 large onions, sliced
1/4 pound boiled ham, cut into thick strips
1/2 teaspoon white pepper and 1/8 teaspoon black pepper
1 teaspoon dried basil

1. Preheat oven to 350°F.
2. In a saucepan, melt 4 tablespoons of the butter over medium heat. Whisk in 1/4 cup of the soy flour and cook, stirring, 2 minutes. Gradually whisk in cream. Bring to a boil and cook, stirring, until thickened; season with white pepper. Remove from heat and stir in Cheddar cheese.

3. Place remaining 1 cup soy flour and black pepper in plastic bag. Add chicken and shake to coat.
4. In a large frying pan, melt remaining 2 tablespoons butter in oil over medium heat. Brown chicken in pan in batches, about 4 minutes on each side; remove to a large roasting pan.
5. Add onions to frying pan and cook 3 minutes, until softened. Add ham, tomatoes, cheese, sauce and basil. Cook 5 minutes. Pour sauce over chicken and cover. Bake 1 hour.
6. Arrange chicken on a large platter. Coat lightly with sauce. Pass remaining sauce separately. Serve warm.

A&B Chicken Santa Maria

2 cups cooked chicken, diced
2 tablespoons butter
2 tablespoons soy flour
1 cup cream (diluted with filtered water), heated
1/2 cup cream
2 tablespoons (dry) sherry
2 egg yolks, beaten
1/2 teaspoon sea salt
1/4 teaspoon white pepper
Dash of hot pepper sauce
1 pinch celery salt

1. In a saucepan, melt butter over medium heat. Stir in flour and cook about 12 minutes, stirring constantly.
2. Gradually whisk in 1 cup cream (diluted with water) and bring to a boil, stirring constantly, until mixture thickens. Reduce heat to low. Add pepper, sea salt, hot pepper sauce.
3. Whisk in 1/2 cup cream. Add sherry and chicken. Season with additional sea salt and pepper to taste. Cook until hot. Remove from heat. Whisk in egg yolks, blending well. Serve warm.

A&B Chicken Liver

1 pound chicken livers
2 tablespoons butter
2 tablespoons olive oil
2 hard-cooked egg yolks
2 medium onions, chopped
1 teaspoon minced garlic
1 teaspoon lemon juice
1/2 teaspoon black pepper
1 teaspoon sea salt

1. Trim chicken livers.
2. Broil chicken livers about 4 inches from heat, turning frequently, until brown outside and no longer pink inside, 5-10 minutes.
3. Meanwhile, in a large skillet, cook onions in butter over medium heat until golden brown, about 10 minutes.
4. Scrape onions and olive oil into a food processor.
5. Add liver, sea salt, and pepper and pulse until coarsely chopped. Add egg yolks and chop to desired consistency. Drizzle lemon juice.
6. Serve with French green beans and butter.

A&B Chicken Nuggets

2-1/2 pounds skinless, boneless chicken breasts, cut into 1-inch pieces
Olive oil
1/2 cup cream
1/4 cup soy flour
1/4 cup grated Parmesan cheese
1 teaspoon paprika
1/2 teaspoon oregano

1. In a large frying pan, heat 1 inch of oil.
2. Meanwhile, put cream in a bowl. In a paper bag, combine flour, Parmesan cheese, paprika, and oregano. Mix well.
3. First dip chicken pieces in cream; then place about a dozen pieces of chicken at a time in bag and shake until they are evenly coated.
4. Fry chicken in hot oil in batches, turning occasionally, for about 5 minutes, until crisp and golden brown. Drain on paper towels, serve hot.

B
Grilled Dishes
& Steaks

T-bone steak, sirloin steak, beef ribs, prime ribs, and any kind of grilled dishes should not be marinated with syrup or sauces containing sugar. Instead, marinate with natural products like lemon, vinegar, wine, cognac, garlic powder, celery salt, sea salt, or pepper or dress with soy flour, mixed with egg yolks.

T-bone steak, sirloin steak, and other steak and grilled dishes can be complimented with grilled tomatoes, onions, peppers, zucchini, mushrooms, and any other vegetable (except potatoes and kale); fried eggs and sour cream with or without chives; herb butter; or other dips that do not contain sugar (see recipes).

Hors d'oeuvres, like avocados with shrimp, are perfect. The dish can be completed with "A&B Power Salad" or any other salads, fruit salad, apple dessert, or any other fruit dessert with whipped cream or ice cream (see recipes).

B

Desserts

Creamy A&B Fruit Dessert

1 pound strawberries, chopped
1 pound raspberries, chopped
1/2 pound peaches, chopped
2 cups heavy cream, whipped
Sweetener

Mix ingredients well and refrigerate.

A&B Apple Dessert

5 medium apples, cored, peeled, and 1/2-inch sliced
Olive oil
Dash cinnamon powder

In a frying pan, heat oil and fry 1/2-inch apple slices until golden brown. Sprinkle cinnamon powder to taste.

Baked A&B Apple

5 apples, peeled
1/2 cup walnuts, coarse-grained, chopped
Sweetener

1. Remove cores from apples. Fill apples with walnuts.
2. Preheat oven to 350°F. Top every apple with a piece of butter. Bake until lightly browned.

Swiss A&B Fruit Salad

1 grapefruit, diced
2 sweet oranges, diced
2 apples, cored, peeled, and sliced in cubes
1 cup pineapple, diced
1 peel of orange, grated
2 cups whipped cream, chilled
1 dash cognac
1 dash cinnamon
Sweetener

In a large bowl, combine all ingredients. Refrigerate for 30 minutes. Serve cool.

B

Ice Cream

A&B Strawberry Ice Cream

(Or Any Other Favorite "B"-fruit)

2 cups heavy cream, whipped
1 pound fruit

1. In a processor, combine whipped cream with fruit.
2. In a plastic bowl, put mixture into freezer and chill at least for 1–1-1/2 hours. Serve with whipped cream. Garnish with fresh fruits.

INDEX